Praise for *Probate & Trust Administration Tips & Tricks*

"I was first introduced to Dan through an attorney. I had taken over a family trust which had several issues that were beyond my area of expertise. After sitting with Dan, I found we share many of the same values enabling me to put my mind at ease. Together we tackled and unraveled the mysteries of the trust and its multiple amendments.

Dan has written this book in such a simple way, that I have used it as a guide, and I recommend to anyone who will or have been put in similar situations - it has revealed many hidden truths of what to expect."

ADRIANNE KORDELOS, Finance, HR, and
Administrative Services Consultant

"Receivership? What the heck is a Receivership? Well, it's a lifesaver is what it is. When my father passed, he was a small business owner in a business that uses heavy equipment. I had my hands full and didn't know where to turn. I had ex-wives, widows, and more laying claims to whatever they thought they could get their hands on. When my Trust Attorney suggested a Receivership, I was confused and concerned. I did not understand how it worked and was terrified to turn over the power of our small company to a complete stranger. Trusting my attorney, I said, OK let's do this. He said it would protect you and your beneficiaries. Within a few days, I met Dan Collins and felt instantly at ease."

"Dan was available to me day and night, and yes even sometimes with a 5:00 am text message. He walked me through all types of issues, and trust me, in my case we have had plenty to choose from. Don't be afraid, my friends. There are actually people out there who care! Dan Collins is one of them."

DARLEAH COX, Oroville, California

"Daniel Collins has written a valuable book for anyone: professional or non-professional to understand how probate and trust administration operates in the United States. Every State will have its particular Probate laws and guidelines. What *Probate & Trust Administration Tip & Tricks* provides is a useful road map to maneuver through the complex administration process. This book is a helpful guide and reference in my practice as a California Licensed Professional Fiduciary as well as for persons stepping into a position as a private or court appointed Administrator for the first time. A fiduciary should always be thinking about liability risk, how to minimize the risks, and what decisions should be made to protect and preserve Estate assets. Management of an Estate no matter the size is subject to the balancing between liability risk and asset preservation, the information in this book provides understanding to professional or non-professional fiduciaries how to perform their duties so risk is minimized. I highly recommend reading this book before beginning Probate or Trust administration."

DEBRA ROSE, JD, CLPF
Owner, Rose Trust & Fiduciary, Folsom, California

"Dear Daniel, I can't thank you enough for your expert assistance in this matter. This latest letter on my behalf to get my attorney fees reimbursed is above and beyond, and something completely unexpected.

I actually am amazed they responded so quickly! After the tone of Charlize's letter I wasn't hopeful, but the attorney finally got it right, as he did with demanding closing of escrow and release of all our funds.

From your initial locating of Dad's 2nd mortgage, which saved us $2,500 on that ridiculous form escrow proposed, to taking the time and effort to reach out to Charlize and the title company on my behalf is something I will never forget. It is friends like you that are the best and most beautiful thing in life. All my best to you always."

LINDA BARBER, Rancho Mirage, California

Probate & Trust Estate Administration Tips & Tricks

ESTATES WITH HOMES AND REAL ESTATE INVESTMENTS

Daniel Collins

Book layout © 2018 BookDesignTemplates.com
Cover design by askaramantra

Names: Daniel, Collins
Title: Probate & Trust Administration Tips & Tricks / by Daniel Collins
Description: 1st ed. | Includes index.
Identifiers: ISBN 978-1-7335145-0-7 (paperback) | ISBN 978-1-7335145-2-1 (e-book)

Printed in the United States of America

This book is dedicated to my wife, Lynn Collins, whose generous spirit supports me in more ways than I can count.

This book is also dedicated to my parents, Mary Ann Collins and Dick Wagner. It was taking care of your respective estates that allowed me to develop systems for what we can never be prepared to do when asked to settle the life affairs of another person.

Daniel Collins, Sacramento, CA
dcollins@collins-commercial.net
(916) 215-2042

Contents

FOREWORD

BY MICHAEL HACKARD, ESQ.

Imagine that your father dies leaving an estate that includes a house that he lived in, and a rental house that your sister is living in, as well as a storage unit filled with decades worth of accumulated objects of all kinds. This happens all the time. You are suddenly presented with a series of issues and questions you are unprepared to answer. It's not your fault. No one ever sees such issues coming, and no can ever prepare for what is to come.

But you still need answers to a series of thorny questions like these:

- Who is going to help you with this estate?
- Who is going to tell you what kind of insurance you need for this estate?
- Who is going to help you deal with your sister, who doesn't want to pay rent?
- What is included in the estate?
- What belongs to each beneficiary and how are family possessions to be split up?

- When do you need to speak to a mortgage lender about selling or keeping the property?
- If your father died in Sacramento, but he had a rental house in San Francisco, where are you going to file a probate?

Then there is a laundry list of "why" questions, starting with:

- Why do you have to do all this?
- Why does the law require this?
- Why does the IRS require this?
- Why will you be responsible for a failed duty if you neglect to take care of filing a probate case?

These are the kind of questions that you will be asking.

Good luck finding the information in a Google search. Or maybe you hope that your attorney will guide you through the process. Unfortunately, as a long-practicing Trust & Estates attorney, I can tell you that most lawyers are ill-equipped to answer these questions, and fewer still will help you resolve them. These are precisely the kind of questions that this book answers.

Dan Collins has straightforward and practical advice for people who are thrust into the uncomfortable position of going to Probate Court for the first time, and who have no idea what to do. This book is your roadmap.

Start here.

Michael Hackard, Esq.
Mather, California

PREFACE

ON RISK

1980

Marin Headlands, California

It is 11:30 p.m., June 27, 1980. I slide into a parking stall at the Golden Gate Bridge lookout parking lot off Highway 1 in the Marin Headlands. Next to me is my girlfriend, Linda, and in the backseat is one of her roommates from the rambling Victorian she shares with four other Cal students on Russell Street in Berkeley, named John. I can hear the engine of my Honda ping as it cools while we wait for my friend Paul to show up. Paul is the real reason I am here; I promised him I would take him on an ascent of the Golden Gate Bridge before I leave for Officer's Candidate School in Quantico, VA. Ever since my first ascent during my senior year in high school, Paul has told me how much he wanted to climb the Golden Gate. This will be my third ascent and my going away present to Paul. He pulls up into the parking space next to my car and shuts down his Volkswagen van which we call "the breadbox."

Why would anyone want to climb to the top of the Golden Gate Bridge? Even veteran climbers, which I considered myself to be, had been known to slip and fall to their deaths off the bridge. Not to mention the fact that climbing the bridge at any time of the day or night was (and still is) illegal. Had I been caught, my Marine Corps career would have been over before it started. But life is about risks – managing risks, calculating risks, taking risks – without which I believe life would have very little meaning.

The view from the top of the Golden Gate Bridge is breath-taking and awe-inspiring, which no photograph can do justice. The risks, in my opinion, greatly outweigh the rewards, and so I am there with my friends to do what few people ever dare to do.

It's technically not a climb, it's a walk up, but those towers are designed to move. The vibration from the vehicles and trucks crossing the bridge, even after midnight in light traffic, causes the towers to literally sway. To add to the challenge of having our path of travel moving side to side is the fact we are in the dark above the bay. Heights are accentuated when you are above water, and the top of the Golden Gate towers are over 700 feet above the water. It can be daunting. But tonight, we had perfect weather conditions, and I had climbed this route in misty fog with light winds before. Tonight's conditions were far better. We reached the top of the cable within 10 or 15 minutes' time. I was first to the top followed by Linda, Paul, and John.

At the top, Paul pulls out his 35mm camera with color film and takes a long exposure picture holding his camera on a 90-degree angle where two steel beams intersect. I keep a framed print from one of his photos in my office to this day, a constant reminder that calculated risks are worth taking.

A Golden Gate Bridge, metaphorically speaking, awaits all of us at some point in our careers. It could be an audacious goal, a seemingly insurmountable challenge, or perhaps a ridiculously hard obstacle. Most people take one look and walk the other way. "Isn't it scary to be up there? Isn't it too difficult? Wouldn't that be dangerous?" Maybe so, but there is no place I would rather be.

Life is a series of risks and adventures, of trial and error, of failure and success. I chose the life I did for the same reasons I climbed the Golden Gate Bridge: To quote the famous poem, Ulysses, by Lord Alfred Tennyson: "To strive, to seek, to find, and not to yield."

In probate and trust matters, problems and struggles will await you at every turn, and it will be easy to get discouraged. At such moments, consider my story of scaling the Golden Gate Bridge and remember that life is an adventure – embrace it.

My days of breaking trespassing laws are long gone, and I certainly would never advise anyone to be stupid or reckless. What survives from those experiences in my own mind is the certain knowledge that intelligent risks can be managed. Experts can guide you, but make sure that they are people you would literally trust with your life; if not, you'll need to look further. Precautions can, and should, always be taken. Expect the best but plan for the worst.

INTRODUCTION

Ｔhis is not a how-to book about administering estates. If you think you want to administer an estate on your own, without the help of qualified professionals to assist you, I hope you will read this book and reconsider that decision. The how-to books on the market give the illusion that "any dummy" can do it. Except in rare cases involving estates with very few moving pieces, that assessment is probably not accurate. It's harder than it looks.

The information contained in this book is based on my 35 years' experience working as a residential and investment real estate broker, general contractor, and land developer in the states of California and Oregon. Since 2009, I have served as a court-appointed receiver administrator. Those litigation skill sets evolved into my helping attorneys in trust litigation matters, and administrators who need an experienced real estate broker to position and sell or distribute, commercial and residential real property assets. In working on cases where disputes arise in probate and trust estates, I have seen many examples of both well-managed and poorly-managed administration. Some extremely bright and seemingly well-qualified people manage to perform poorly.

The stories I tell in this book are meant to demonstrate common themes of what I have seen and learned in administering probate and trust estates. The stories of litigation in probate and trust matters have been altered to protect client privilege, as is my duty as an officer of the court.

In a litigation case I consulted on in the past, I was presented with a young man who was an artist by trade. He was made the trustee of a trust shortly before his wife's grandfather passed away. When the grandfather died, he became the successor trustee. This was an accommodation of love to support his wife. She had a demanding professional job and the hours she worked made it impractical for her to perform the task of administering the estate, so her husband stepped in. They were concerned about the grandfather's son being the successor trustee upon his death. The reason for concern was based upon his uncle's drug addiction.

Substance abuse is one of the single most common problems I deal with in assisting people in administering estates. Beneficiaries with substance abuse issues can cause estate administration to be very burdensome. The young man had no experience in business, and that lack of experience also caused him all kinds of problems. I had originally been brought in to help him with real property issues, but it quickly became obvious to me that he didn't understand some of the basic steps that were required to administer the estate. For example, he didn't know that he had to notify the Social Security Administration that his wife's grandfather had passed away -- four months had already gone by. Even the process of opening a checking account for the trust was completely beyond him, because it's not easy opening fiduciary bank accounts due to government regulations that banking institutions must comply with after 9/11.

I dug in and worked to assist the young man with administering the estate he had unwittingly agreed to administer without having any idea of the burdens and risks it entailed. That allowed him to re-start the process correctly, albeit a bit late, but it put him on the best trajectory to properly settle the estate correctly, which supported his good standing in litigation, too.

Even people who have significant business experience are sometimes not qualified to administer an estate. In another case, a man inherited a small business from his father, and he was more than capable of running the business. What he was not equipped for, however, was dealing with all the creditors who made claims against the business and his father. He was deluged with claimants who were making things up and trying to extract money, and he had no idea how to deal with that situation. Sometimes people need an experienced professional to stand by them and serve as a gatekeeper to require people to prove up their claims.

This book is intended to be an aerial view of the estate and probate settlement process. Once you see the scope of how the process works, I hope you will decide to hire professionals who are equipped to guide you through the maze of forms, procedures, and hearings. Being an executor or trustee of an estate is a totally thankless job. If you have already been called upon to do the job, you will probably do everything in your power to avoid doing it a second time.

My purpose in writing this book is to provide you with an overview of what to expect, and provide advice for getting through the process. The probate and estate administration process is in many ways a relic from the past, but it is a relic that nevertheless serves a useful purpose for society. You might hope, for example, that Probate Courts would streamline their procedures and make use of new technologies. Such is unlikely to be the case for a very long time. The probate process may eventually evolve, but change comes very slowly to arcane and byzantine systems. Before you delve in, and before you become hopelessly frustrated with the archaic world of trusts and probate, I hope this book will serve as fair warning to find and hire the best qualified professional advocates and assistants.

If you are being called upon to be an executor of an estate or a trustee of a trust, a quick read of this book is a good idea because it will give you a solid idea of what to expect.

If you are involved in any level of dispute or resulting litigation, the book may also help you to understand how others have dealt with situations similar to your own. Heirs and beneficiaries are frequently in some economic distress, and those people often put pressure on the administrator or trustee to make quick decisions, sometimes decisions that are not in the best interest of the estate. If that's your situation, I hope that this book will also persuade you to hire competent gatekeepers and professionals who can manage expectations for combative heirs and beneficiaries and take some of the emotional burden off you.

I also hope that attorneys, paralegals, accountants, bookkeepers, professional fiduciaries, and the vast array of people who provide services to estates, may also get some benefit from this book, as it may help provide some perspective on what it feels like to be in the shoes of an administrator. The day to day requirements of administering an estate can be stressful and complex. Each professional understands his or her own area of specialization, of course, but few of those professionals go through each step in the process. I have administered estates from start to finish and have helped many others through various parts of the process.

Above all, I feel great empathy for those who are required to serve, and hope that this book will give them encouragement and support.

Dan Collins
Sacramento, California

1

Making Arrangements Upon Death

Before you call Social Security, before you call a lawyer, before you file a probate, before you start notifying all the people who will want or need to know that someone has passed on, your very first job as the future executor, or personal representative, or trustee of an estate, is **to focus on the practical but uncomfortable aspects of someone's death**. Assuming the person who died has left written or reliable verbal instructions about their wishes with respect to the disposition of their body, burial or cremation, funeral services and/or a "celebration of life" amongst family and friends, your job is to carry out those last wishes. There are, of course, reasonable conditions, like having the financial resources available to cover the expenses.

Arranging for funeral services typically involves several common options. Will the loved be buried or cremated?

Burial is the traditional choice. It can be done directly, with no viewing or ceremonies, or with any combination of viewing, ceremony, and graveside service. It usually requires you to pay for a casket, cemetery plot; fees to open and close the grave; cemetery maintenance; and a grave marker or headstone. Most burials are below ground. The other option is burial above ground in a mausoleum; this option often is more expensive.

Cremation is a popular preference for people in the United States. It also offers flexibility, requiring neither a casket nor embalming. There is flexibility as to when or where services are held; many families now hold memorial services in their own homes or at a predetermined favorite place of the deceased's. The deceased's last instructions or preference may involve a viewing, and ceremony followed by cremation. Some funeral homes offer rental caskets for cremation, while others sell modest caskets designed for cremation. Cremation is often the least expensive of common methods for disposition of the body.

If a religious service is part of the deceased's last wishes and they were active in a church, synagogue or other religious affiliation, that is where you will likely want to make arrangements for a service consistent with the faith of loved one. Typically, there are no set costs for faith services, but it is customary that a donation to be made to the church, synagogue or another place of worship by the family or friends.

If the deceased is a military veteran, the Veterans Administration will provide a burial plot at a national veterans' national cemetery and based upon eligibility, may provide an allowance for funeral costs. The family may choose to have military funeral honors. This may include the playing of "Taps," a rifle detail, a color guard, or uniformed Service Members who present the burial flag.

ESTIMATING COSTS

Regardless of which option the deceased prefers for disposition of their body, funeral service or celebration of life event, you need to plan and estimate the costs associated with carrying out the last wishes of the deceased. If catering services for food or beverages will be involved, include those costs in your estimate. Keep in mind, if you are the person responsible for settling the estate as a Personal Representative or Trustee, you should keep the costs in line with the anticipated value of the deceased's estate.

Sometimes budgeting for last wishes to be carried out means you must help other family members or friends understand that there are limited financial resources. Settling an estate definitely entails costs, and you are responsible for managing the estate's financial resources. And, it is not uncommon when people live to old age that they are "cash poor and asset rich" at the time of death. Since the disposition of the body and funeral or celebration of life services most often occur within a short period of time to the date of death, you need to focus on the availability of cash resources.

WHAT IF THERE'S NO MONEY AVAILABLE?

This happens. Assuming the deceased had an estate of sufficient value and was not indigent, you may still find yourself faced with no cash resources to carry out the last wishes. I have been involved in estate litigation cases and real estate brokerage services to market and sell estate owned homes and income property where there literally was no cash left in the deceased bank or brokerage accounts. I had a case recently where the deceased had been cremated but there was no money available to pay and re-patriate their remains, it took nine months to liquidate trust assets sufficient to pay the funeral home and secure the decedent's cremated remains.

I work with a licensed fiduciary who told me of a case she had where the body was left in the morgue for over four months, and she had to fight to prevent the local govern-ment from disposing of the remains. These situations of zero cash resources do occur, and they can really prevent you from executing the last wishes of the deceased. If you find yourself in this situation, start thinking about impro-vising.

You may need to ask family members to chip in, or you may be persuaded to lend the estate or trust your own money. A word of caution about using your own money to cover estate expenses: I often work with people who are administering an estate, and they use their own funds as a "loan" to cover estate expenses with the expectation they will be reimbursed from the proceeds of liquidating the es-tate. I will get into this more in later chapters, but for now, I will simply recommend that you do not do that. If you elect to do it anyway, then do not expect to reimburse yourself until your fiduciary obligations to the estate have been met, or you may find yourself in trouble with benefi-ciaries or the Probate Court. If you want to learn more on this topic, please skip ahead to Chapter 13: When Trustees or Personal Representatives Loan Money to an Estate.

CHAPTER SUMMARY:

- As a first step, do your best to honor the last wishes of the deceased.

- Consider the finances and resources of the estate before committing to expensive options.
- **<u>Do not lend money</u>** to the estate unless you are willing to ultimately consider it a gift or long-term loan because, in most cases, it will be one or the other.

2

Find the Will – And Why You Probably Need to Hire a Private Investigator

In almost every case, a person's will is the crucial document that guides the process of settling an estate. If everyone kept an up to date will, and if everyone made sure that signed and notarized copies were readily available, things would go smoothly.

Unfortunately, things hardly ever go smoothly...

Let's start with the fact that wills frequently disappear. In my experience, 15-20% of the time there are problems with either finding a Will that heirs believe exists, finding a current will or finding a will (or Living Trust) that hasn't been tampered with. The incidence of such problems with wills and trust documents is roughly comparable to the incidence of "undue influence." These are cases where elderly people are taken advantage of financially, or a beneficiary takes advantage of the elderly's stated wishes for the disposition of their estate at the end of their lives, so they can enrich themselves at the cost of robbing other beneficiaries of their rightful inheritance.

When there are bad actors involved they will generally do a couple of things: Sometimes they "amend" documents to include information that clearly doesn't look authentic. Other times a new will document mysteriously and miraculously appears.

Here are a few basic facts you should know about wills:

- You'll need an original document, which is signed and either notarized or has a witness - preferably both.
- If you can't find an original document, a copy (signed or otherwise) may be submitted to the Probate Court, but it will be entirely up to a Probate Judge whether to accept the document.
- If someone dies without a will (called 'In Testate'), there are accepted rules for inheritance that will guide the distribution of assets: Children are generally first in line to inherit on an equal basis. After that come siblings and parents.
- If there is no will and no direct descendants, the estate will generally be taken by the State.

If the Trustee or Personal Representative had a close relationship with the decedent, that often makes things easier. However, I've been involved in cases where the Personal Representative or Trustee had no idea what was going on in the decedent's financial world - literally no information at all about what was going on with them financially. If you are not intimately familiar with the decedent, the challenges become commensurate with the lack of relationship.

A Trustee's first and most important jobs are:

- Find the will - if there is one. Whether it's a probate or trust case, the will is always the first step.
- Identify and inventory all assets that are part of the estate; time is of the essence to complete this task.
- Identifying and inventory all liabilities/debts that are part of the estate.
- Take control of all assets to prevent theft or misappropriation.

Since your first and most important job will be to 'find the will,' you will need to use any and all means possible to accomplish that job:

- Go through every drawer.
- Look at every file.
- Is there a safety deposit box at the bank where the decedent had checking and other accounts?
- Locate every financial record you can find.
- Search their computer for all relevant documents and files.
- Sometimes you're going to need to go through boxes up in the attic or the basement.
- Find past years' tax returns, if they are available. Tax returns can be very helpful in identifying assets.

The problem with wills and trusts is that they are not recorded public documents. There could potentially be Memorandums recorded at the local County Recorder's

Office somewhere, stating the existence of a will or trust, but that is very rare.

YOU PROBABLY SHOULD CONSIDER HIRING A PRIVATE INVESTIGATOR

Finding a will sounds simple enough, but it can and does often literally turn into an investigation. Unfortunately, most people who are thrown into the role of settling an estate or trust are unqualified to conduct a proper investigation. If you don't have good computer skills, if you don't have good financial and accounting skills, if you aren't detail oriented, and especially if you aren't completely current and intimately familiar with a decedent's financial affairs, I strongly advise you to consider hiring a licensed private investigator (PI). And, if you are a beneficiary or heir, and you don't know the person who is administering the estate from which you expect to inherit, you too may want to consider doing a thorough background check on that person.

As you're reading this, you probably have in mind a somewhat outdated vision of what a private investigator does. I am not talking about a PI who wears a fedora and surreptitiously follows suspects with a camera. In fact, most private investigators in business these days spend more time in front of a computer than a camera.

Why would you want to hire a private investigator? Here are a few good reasons:

- A PI can do some background checking on all potential heirs, caregivers, friends, or anyone else who may have been a part of the decedent's financial life.

- A PI can also help identify people who had financial dealings with vulnerable elders, e.g., caregivers or dependent adult children who substituted their choices or desires for the decedents' own if they were incapacitated before they passed – this is known as undue influence and elder abuse.
- A trained and competent PI will likely find all sorts of documentation that most people may never know existed.
- A PI may find business relationships you didn't know existed.
- A PI can identify interests in negotiable instruments - e.g., real property or a private loan that may have been made.
- Sometimes background information can give you a trail that helps you to locate the will and find assets that aren't readily identifiable in a decedent's files.

If it sounds expensive, you should know that it generally isn't. A basic background check by a PI will often take them a few hours of time and cost less than $200. Private investigators hourly rate will often range from $40-$100 per hour. If a wider search involving more people and documents is needed, a search may run closer to $500.

My advice would be to hire a private investigator who is a retired law enforcement official (FBI or Police Detective), some of whom will have decades of experience. Yes, it could be a zero-sum event if the person you hire doesn't find anything more than what you could discover on your own with hard copies of records and files. But if there is not a good document history, or if the document history is in disarray, that's when you should contemplate looking for outside help at that level.

Do you need permission to hire a PI? If you are the Trustee of the estate or the Personal Representative, then the answer is no. You own the decedent's property until it is distributed to the estate's beneficiaries. You have a fiduciary responsibility to care and preserve it for the beneficiaries. You are always allowed, as necessary, in your role as a Trustee or Personal Representative, to hire competent professionals to assist you in administering the estate or trust and charge those expenses to the estate.

How would you find a good PI? If you don't already know one, and chances are you don't, you should look for people who currently or previously taught classes in private investigation. In California (and most states), there is a professional organization of licensed private investigators: http://www.cali-pi.org/. For starters, you should make sure that whomever you choose is a licensed member. A quick search of "Probate" and "Probate/Missing Heirs" using their search page turned up more than 120 qualified companies. You can narrow the search based on criteria that may matter to you, such as specific geographic location or specific sub-specialty expertise.

If you end up spending $500, is it going to be worth it to hire a PI? In my opinion, the answer is almost always 'yes.' The basic searches such people can do for you is like looking for low hanging fruit. More than likely, the information you uncover will be worth the cost.

As the sole caregiver for someone who died, you have been paying bills and filing their taxes for years, in which case a PI may not be able to tell you much more than you already know. By the time my mother died, for example, I had been taking care of her finances for five years, and I knew the full extent of her financial assets and liabilities. I decided not to hire an investigator because I was quite certain I knew she hadn't set up an offshore bank account or had assets I was unaware of.

Even in cases such as mine, however, there is always the chance that a PI might discover a long-lost account in another State that inadvertently became 'abandoned property.' If only for the peace of mind, it can be extremely helpful to have a 3rd party corroborate or verify that you aren't missing anything of importance. If the estate has cash and the resources to spend a few hundred dollars, I believe this is often an investment worth making.

MORE REASONS TO SEEK OUTSIDE HELP
If you are the Trustee or Personal Representative of an Estate, there will be no substitute for you going through all the financial documents available to you. But especially if finances are not your strong suit, you should certainly look to get outside help. While it may cost more, a PI or a bookkeeper can also be hired to physically go through a decedent's files and papers to locate important documents and records. As we get older, we tend to become more disorganized and misfile things. Sometimes people who have been hired as caregivers can 'lose' important documents. Either way, it helps to know what you are looking for, and sometimes what information did not immediately turn up.

Why is it so important to find the paper trail? As a rule, if you are the successor Trustee or the Personal Representative of an Estate, one of your first jobs will be to immediately identify all checking, saving and investment accounts, and both notify the financial institutions that the holder of the account has died, and provide them with a death certificate. What happens then is that the institutions will freeze the accounts until you can provide Letters of Testamentary if it's a probate, or with a trust that you can show that you are the successor Trustee and have a Certification of both the trust as well as Certification that you are the Successor Trustee.

Suppose that your investigations lead you to believe that there are undiscovered assets, or perhaps that someone was exerting 'undue influence' upon the decedent. In that case, you may decide that a larger budget beyond $500 is warranted to learn more. In such cases, it is always a judgment call. How much could be gained, and at what cost? Do the potential benefits outweigh the potential costs? You can only answer that on a case by case basis.

What about background checks on people who were near and dear to the person who died? Should you investigate the caregivers or friends? Again, there are no black and white answers, but if you suspect that fraud has occurred, if there are missing assets, if there are missing records, or if you notice anything unusual about the handling of finances then, yes, it may be worth it to dig a little more into the lives of people who were there at the end, especially if you were not. Did the nurse have a gambling problem? Was the friendly next-door neighbor who paid the bills siphoning off money for himself? When the car got sold by Uncle Dave, what happened to the money? If you suspect there may have been instances of elder financial abuse or undue influence, these are things that may be discovered by hiring the right professional.

In sum, if you haven't already been directly involved in someone's financial affairs for a long time before they passed away, don't assume that you know everything that's important to know about their estate. For a very modest investment, which I would advise capping at $500, make your first decision to hire a competent private investigator. What you don't know may end up costing you a lot more in the long run. Beyond that, you will also have performed your fiduciary duty for standards of practice to identify Trust assets and estate obligations. Whatever liability you might be assuming just by being an Estate Administrator or Trustee (which we'll discuss in a later chapter) will be greatly reduced by taking this one small, first step.

Remember, Personal Representatives and Trustees are allowed by Law to use estate assets to hire competent professionals to perform the tasks and duties that they are themselves not qualified to perform - and it is incumbent upon them to do that. Competency in administering an estate through probate or trust is a higher standard of expertise than most people realize. Truthfully, few individuals will ever have all the necessary experience to address the scope of administering an estate.

CHAPTER SUMMARY:

- Finding a will, if there is one, is a critical first step.
- Hiring a Private Investigator will, in most cases, pay for itself in multiple ways.
- Do not be afraid to reach out for help.
- As the fiduciary of someone's estate, you will have an obligation to meet certain standards.
- If you need assistance, the estate will cover the cost of hiring professionals.

3

Settling a Trust Estate

The benefit of having a Living Trust, which becomes irrevocable upon a person's death, is that you can immediately start the process of distribution of assets to beneficiaries. Whereas by comparison, in a probate you are not allowed to take any action until the Probate Court issues Letters of Testamentary either appointing you as the Personal Representative or an Administrator if you are not named in the decedent's Will. When there is no Will to be found, the Court will appoint an Administrator, who is often a professional (like a Licensed Fiduciary) or, a qualified family member, to administer the estate in probate. Probate is a lot more cumbersome to administer, by comparison to administering a Trust Estate.

Even with a Trust, not all assets owned by the decedent may be in the name of the trust. In older Trust documents, if you don't specifically add asset titles into the name of the Trust, they're not treated as trust assets and therefore may be subject to probate. For example, you might not have the title of your primary residence in the Trust, thinking it is already covered. That's an oversight lots of people make. If the decedent re-financed the home after they formed their Living Trust, lenders frequently require their loan documents to be in a legal person's name, not the name of a trust. Consequently, a home that was once in the name of your trust is now in your personal name after refinancing the property. You can protect your home as a trust asset when refinancing but you must be proactive and ask to keep the title in the name of the trust. Or, after securing the new loan, go back and record another deed to the property in the name of the trust.

Guess what? If the home is not specifically noted as being in the Trust, and you have an older trust document without a "pour-over clause," your house may be subject to the probate process. What is a "pour-over clause"? Talk to your trust attorney about this point of law; a pour-over will transfer, or "pours," any property belonging to an individual at the time of his death into his existing trust. That alone is reason enough to consider updating a Living Trust on a periodic basis, known as a Restatement of Trust, - just to make sure that it will cover what you want.

Normally, in the reading of the Trust or the reading of a Will, it is usually clear if there is a 'pour over clause' which allows assets that are not specifically named in the Trust to be included in the Trust. *If the Trust you are administering does not have a 'pour-over clause' that adds all settlor assets into the trust, you could find yourself administering both a trust and a probate estate(s) for one decedent.*

So why can't someone just sell a piece of real estate without having to go through a cumbersome probate process like they can with a Trust? Even though you might, technically, be able to transfer title without settling a probate estate, as a practical matter, you will not be able to obtain title insurance insuring good and equitable title to a buyer without either going through probate and having court authority to legally convey equitable title to the property. Hopefully, if you are tasked with administering a trust estate you will not find yourself also having to also administer a probate due to one or more assets were not specifically titled in the name of the trust, and the trust document lacked the 'pour-over clause.'

I was hired as a real estate consultant by an attorney in a Trust litigation case where a woman who had died with a Living Trust owned several properties. The decedent had a 'pour over clause' in her Trust. However, when she drafted her Revocable Living Trust, she owned a home where her mother lived, and she forgot to include that home as a Trust owned asset. When she later died, the attorney representing the Trustee filed a California Probate Code 850 Petition (this type of application is commonly referred to as a Heggstad Petition) to seek the transfer of title of 'Granny's house' into the Trust. The court rejected the request to bring 'Granny's house' into the Trust, even though the Trust had a 'pour-over clause' because the decedent owned "Granny's house" before the formation of the Trust. That oversight by the original Settler who created the Trust caused the Trustee's counsel to petition the court for probate to bring 'Granny's house' into the Trust. This mistake by the Trustee's mom, who was the Settlor, caused a delay to complete the Trust distribution and closure for almost nine months. A heavy burden for her daughter who was the sibling burdened with serving as the Trustee to settle her mother's estate.

The following scenario is common - more so than you might think: The trigger is when someone tries to sell assets from an estate. Suppose Uncle Joe died in 1998 and his family continued to live in his house, still titled in Uncle Joe's name, for 20 years after his death. The family finally decides they want to sell Uncle Joe's house. They hire a real estate agent, they go under contract of sale, they open an escrow account with a title company, and the title company searches the title history and discovers that the house is still titled to Uncle Joe and that it was never taken through probate. At that point, the title company will explain that they can't insure title to the contracted property buyer because the seller(s) don't have legal title.

To gain legal title, the heir(s) need to go to Court, file a will (if there is one), or file a petition intestate (if there is no will). At that point, it will be a matter of legal statute for the court to determine who the legal heirs are. Eventually, title to the property will be transferred to the beneficiary, but that process will still require probate - which means Letters of Testamentary. It is possible for there to be a delay - even a very long delay that stretches into decades - but there is no way around the probate process unless assets are owned by a Trust. Remember, to legally transfer title to real property in an estate you will always need:

- A certified death certificate
- Letters of Testamentary, or
- Letters of Administration, or if a Trust,
- Certification of Trust document and Certification of Trustee

DIFFERENT LEVELS OF AUTHORITY GRANTED BY THE PROBATE COURT

There are several different levels of authorities a Court can grant:

- Full Authority - which means that the Letter of Testamentary will state that "Eric Smith" is considered to be the Personal Representative of the Estate of John Doe, and has full authority to distribute assets of that estate.
- Limited Authority - which means that you can go under contract for the sale of real property or real estate, but those sales are subject to review and approval by the Court. This step could add between a month to several months in the time to get a sale transaction completed.
- Blocked Accounts - which means that the Court gives very limited authority and exclude someone from transacting any business without specific authority of the Court. This is the most cumbersome level of authority.

Keep in mind that with Limited Authority and Blocked Accounts, delays in getting Court approval to sell real property or to liquidate investment accounts should be expected. Getting on a Court's docket can add one to several months to any process. Nothing happens quickly in probate when court approval is required!

Real property is probably one of the most common and highly documented assets that are transferred from estates. The need to transfer a title that is both "good and equitable" that a title insurance company will stand behind and insure such title, ultimately forces everyone to comply with probate requirements if the real property was not in the name of a trust.

If you are a family member who is named as the Personal Representative of the probate estate and you are given full authority in your Letters of Testamentary you are in the best position possible to complete the administration of the estate. The one thing you want to do as soon as you receive your Letters of Testamentary is to send out your required Notice to Creditors. The notice must be published three times in a periodical, usually a local newspaper suffices, and you want to mail the court's approved form Notice to Creditor to utility companies, credit card companies, and other accounts the decedent maintained. The California statutory period to allow creditors to makes claims against the estate is four months, so you want to get started as soon as possible to commence your creditor notice requirements. Not properly executing the statutory notice to creditors correctly can cause significant time delays to closing out the estate and making distributions to heirs.

The advantage of having property placed in a Trust is clear: If you own a house in the name of the "John Doe 1993 Trust" and the title to the property reads that way, and you have a Death Certificate, and you have a certificate of Trust that an attorney has prepared, with you certified as being the Trustee, that will often suffice for a title company to insure the title and agree to insure equitable title via a deed transfer at time of sale.

Even if you have a Living Trust, it may still not be quick or easy to transfer title to a property that is not titled in the exact name of the trust. If the name on the property was just "John Doe," and not "John Doe Trust" then the title insurance company may require you to go to Court to get documentation that proves your authority to lawfully transfer title. That process is likely to take many months.

As a side note, you should know those title insurance companies tend to take their jobs very seriously. In the case of a single-family home transfer, they will search out any liens that may exist on the property, they will make sure that all the property taxes have been paid, and then they will determine whether utility easements are in good standing. Their number one responsibility is to insure equitable title, to do that they must make sure that title to the property is held correctly before, during and after any transaction.

ARE YOU QUALIFIED TO SETTLE AN ESTATE?
What sort of qualifications do you need to settle an estate? As with being a parent, there are no prerequisites. While anyone can do it, that doesn't mean everyone is equally qualified.

You should think of estate management as being like a business. Whether it's a trust or probate, the skills required to competently administer the estate are pretty much the same. You need to be able to have some understanding of business, keep track of expenses, be able to open a checking account, get a Tax ID number, identify the estate's assets and obligations, notify potential creditors, and you must be prepared to file a tax return for the decedent as well as a fiduciary tax return for the trust.

If you don't file your own taxes or don't know anything about filing taxes, I strongly advise you to hire an accountant or bookkeeper who can assist you. Whether a probate or trust estate, when someone dies the estate itself must obtain a new tax ID number and must file taxes. Misunderstanding tax laws can cause an estate to grossly overpay or underpay taxes, and it's not usually worth taking the risk that you can do it yourself online with tax prep software.

Since the Trump Tax Law in 2018 estates are not taxed unless they exceed ten million dollars in value, so as a practical matter, not many estates today have to be concerned with estate taxes at the federal level. States may have their own and separate treatment of inheritance taxation.

You will also need to know which assets you can and cannot immediately distribute and identify what falls under probate or trust and what assets don't. For example, if there is an investment account and the 'Joe Smith 1993 Trust' owns it with his grandson, that's a joint account with right of survivorship, which immediately goes to that beneficiary and does not become part of the estate. If that account just read 'Joe Smith 1993 Trust' without any other named beneficiaries, then that would become part of the estate and would be distributed to all the beneficiaries of the estate.

In many cases, the way estate assets are handled is subject to some discretion and judgment, which means that you may be required to make hard decisions that may prove to be unpopular with beneficiaries. Your estranged brother, Fred, may feel that he's getting a raw deal, whether true or not, which may cause Fred to hire an attorney to harass you until you do what Fred wants! If that sounds bad, it is. Most people think of themselves as being fair-minded and even-handed, but in matters of settling an estate, your perception may differ dramatically from the other beneficiaries. If relations were already strained before, the process of estate settlement will generally make things worse.

You should know that being the Trustee or Personal Representative of an estate is a huge burden. It will take an enormous amount of time, even under the best of circumstances, and it will put strains and stress on relationships you probably never imagined. If a Trust puts obligations on one family member to manage or take care of another, a not uncommon situation, those stresses will only be magnified.

WHEN YOU NEED HELP WITH ESTATE ADMINISTRATION

The inequity of being tasked with being a Trustee or Probate Personal Representative is that you will be 'thrown into the fire' with no warning, no preparation, and no training. You will be saddled with obligations you didn't expect, and you will be held to a legal standard of being a fiduciary that you don't know how to navigate. Problems will come up that you didn't expect and won't know how to resolve. The personal risks of carrying out your fiduciary duties are palpable. The more you know about administering estates the more you recognize the significant personal risk Trustees and Personal Representatives are placed in.

When you don't know what you don't know about administering probate or Trust estates, and you elect to do without legal counsel or tax counsel, you're playing Russian roulette with a loaded pistol. There are plenty of books and online videos available that can help you understand estate administration, but if you conclude that you are a) not qualified or b) not interested or c) not able for whatever reason to serve as a Trustee or Personal Representative, the good news is that you don't have to take the job! Indeed, there are numerous resources available for families that want an independent, professional 3rd party to administer and equitably distribute assets.

The advantage of hiring a "licensed fiduciary" are multiple:

- An expert in estate administration is less likely to make mistakes.
- A 3rd party who has no 'axes to grind,' and who is viewed as impartial, can make the hard distribution choices based upon equity versus influence. If you're worried about long-term relationships, hiring a fiduciary places someone else besides you squarely in the cross-hairs.
- Fiduciaries can save estates time and money because they know ways to maximize asset values and minimize estate liabilities.
- Fiduciaries will, in most cases, be able to settle an estate much faster than a named Trustee or Personal Representative because they know the system and won't waste time.

If you were named as the Trustee of a Living Trust and decided for any reason that you weren't up for the job, you can substitute a professional and licensed Trustee to take over for you. In cases where Trust assets are complex or complicated in any way, that's usually a good idea. To make that happen, you need to petition the Court to do a succession to a professional Trustee, not named specifically in the Trust. The Court will then look at that person's qualifications and approve them or not, or may approve them subject to a performance bond, which means that the professional must ethically administer the estate. The bond itself is a 'performance guarantee' that the professional will not defraud the estate or abscond with any of the estate assets.

I strongly recommend experienced, independent, licensed estate administrators, whether in probate or a trust, hire competent legal counsel to help settle the estate, and you might think that having an attorney to oversee matters will be sufficient. Trust me when I tell you that it won't! Attorneys will make sure that appropriate documents are filed, but whether Aunt Martha's teacup collection goes to Mary, Jane or Sue, or whether the teacup collection gets liquidated with the proceeds split among all beneficiaries, is usually a judgment call. And, why pay attorney's fees to divvy up personal family mementos? How do you decide? Who decides? What happens when someone objects? Do not count on a probate attorney, billing $400 or more per hour, to take an interest in such matters. The details of settling an estate are way beyond the time, and scope of work attorneys normally take on.

You can use a licensed fiduciary to help you, as opposed to becoming a Probate Personal Representative or a Successor Trustee yourself. It is not only OK to hire professionals to assist you, but you *should* hire professionals with steps that you are not qualified to execute yourself. You can pay for all those services from the estate, and as the Trustee or Personal Representative, you have full legal authority to do that.

Often beneficiaries may be critical of you spending money on those types of services, but they're not the ones with the personal liability and responsibility of administering the estate. And, if you or any of the heirs and beneficiaries think there is no personal risk in performing estate administration you are mistaken. What most people don't realize is that being a Trustee or Personal Representative comes with a great deal of personal liability and no insurance, which puts personal assets at risk.

A licensed fiduciary is covered by E&O coverage which is not available to private Trustees or Personal Representatives. When you act in those capacities, you are acting as the fiduciary for all the beneficiaries of the estate. Fiduciaries, whether professional or not, are held to a high legal standard. Any mistakes you make, whether intentional or inadvertent, could cause one or more of the beneficiaries to sue you personally. If you think that would never happen to you and with your family, think again!

It's not just the heirs to a billion-dollar hotel chain that ends up in Court - lots of suits come from estates with total assets of between $250K and $500K. In fact, if you do decide to accept being a Personal Representative or Trustee to administer an estate, I recommend you call your insurance agent and investigate obtaining errors and omissions insurance coverage to protect yourself from any claims by beneficiaries that may cause you to end up in litigation defending your actions.

How do you protect yourself? Hire qualified professionals to assist you at every step along the way. Hire a CPA to file the taxes, hire a licensed appraiser or real estate broker to determine the precise value of real estate assets, hire a licensed contractor to make repairs, and hire a licensed fiduciary to help you maximize the estate's assets so that you can make the distributions to the beneficiaries after you settle the debts and obligations of the estate.

Of course, it's not necessarily as easy as it sounds. Maybe the attorney you hire isn't that good; maybe the CPA is sloppy, etc. As in life, there are no guarantees that by hiring someone you're going to always have a positive result. All along the way, you will want to interview several qualified candidates, get referrals from multiple people, and check references! Before you hire anyone, make sure you call and talk to as many people who have used them as possible. Ask them what problems they encountered, ask them if they know someone who is better. Ask them what problems they should have foreseen.

Ultimately, once you've hired your team, you may need to rely on other professionals to keep tabs on your choices. A CPA may be able to tell you if the bookkeeper is doing a good job. A bookkeeper may be able to notice that a licensed contractor is overcharging. A good attorney may be able to tell you if the licensed fiduciary is handling all the necessary details. If you don't ask, don't assume that people will tell you. Always be willing to ask the hard questions.

Finally, you should know that any disputes, whether there is or is not a Trust, will lead you to a Probate Court. If, for example, a Will is being challenged by a beneficiary or, multiple beneficiaries, a Court must decide how assets are to be divided. Often, court challenges by or amongst beneficiaries, are cases where there is potentially 'undue influence' and/or possible elder financial abuse. Even if there was a Trust that held all the assets, a suspicion of abuse or fraud will inevitably put the matter of dispute in Probate Court, and if that happens, you will need a very good attorney to help navigate through that process.

CHAPTER SUMMARY:

- In a Trust Estate, to gain legal title to a piece of real estate, it will need to be in the name of the trust. If it is not, it may be necessary to go through a probate process. Trying to avoid that will, ultimately, prove useless. No title insurance company will insure title to property that has not been legally probated if it is not in the trust name.

- There are different levels of authority granted by Probate Courts. You need to understand what the differences are, and what you will or will not be able to do without Court approval.
- Being a personal representative, executor or trustee isn't for everyone. There's no shame in admitting that you aren't qualified or simply don't have the time. Either way, you need to know what you're getting yourself in for.
- Regardless of circumstances, always find and hire qualified professionals to assist. You may think you're saving money by doing it yourself, but you may be valuing your own time very cheaply.

4

Settling a Probate Estate

The word "Probate" may mean little or nothing to you, but you should know that the word and the apparatus of Probate Court are all about the concept of "Proving Up." The Probate Estate process is designed to Prove Up a last will and testament of the deceased, Prove Up the estate assets, Prove Up obligations to creditors, and Prove Up values of assets prior to distribution. Don't go into Probate Court under the false assumption that the value of assets doesn't matter. Quite the opposite - the Probate Court system has well-established procedures in place to make sure that a decedent's estate assets are valued prior to distribution to heirs and beneficiaries. The court's process of valuation is not always in alignment with the standards of best practices, but it is well established. Proof is always a necessary and essential part of the process.

The process itself is fairly straightforward and is well covered in lots of books on the subject. My only advice is never to take this job on yourself! Always hire a competent

Probate Attorney at the very start. Ask around, get references, do your homework, and find an attorney who has a great reputation and a lot of experience. The paperwork involved in settling a probate estate can be significant, and the steps that need to be taken will go much more smoothly when a trained professional is handling the case. Unless you have a law degree yourself, and even if you do, you will nearly always be better off hiring experts in probate. You will need to provide a certified copy of the Death Certificate and an original copy of the Last Will and Testament to your attorney. I recommend using your legal counsel to file the necessary petitions and motions for submittal to the Probate Court.

Which isn't to say that you shouldn't know all about the process, what to expect, and how to manage a probate estate. First off, if you are tasked with administering a probate, versus administering a Trust, there are different levels of authority that the Court may grant you as a Personal Representative. The levels will be dependent partly on the value of the estate and partly on the Court's assessment of the skills and ability of the proposed Personal Representative or Administrator for the probate. As noted in the preceding chapter, the different levels are typically Complete or Full Authority, which can be granted either with or without a performance bonding requirement.

Often when people write wills and they stipulate who they want as the Personal Representative to settle their estate, they will often stipulate that they want no bond to be required because it's an additional burden upon the person who has to administer the estate. But the Court will ultimately make that judgment whether to grant full authority, with or without bond requirements.

The other level of authority granted to a Personal Representative by the court may be Limited Authority. The limitations are usually tied to the disposition of higher value assets, such as real estate assets or large investments. When the court grants Limited Authority, the disposition, or sale, of high-value assets must be approved by the Court prior to completion of the sale transaction. An agreement to terms of sale may be entered into by the Personal Representative subject to court review and approval. If you think this is unfair, guess what? In Probate Court, whatever the judge decides is the way things will go. You might disagree that you don't need review and approval from the Court, but while in court, you should keep such opinions to yourself!

If you are granted partial authority, you simply make the best of it. Limited Authority is a time burden because once you have received an acceptable offer on a home or investment property from a Buyer, you must petition the court for a date to review and approve, or disapprove of the terms of the sale. The Court will not be looking to derail your sale; it will instead want to satisfy itself of the following: 1) That the sale terms are consistent and within 90% of the asset value submitted to the court. 2) That the terms of the sale protect the estate after the transaction is completed. 3) That the proposed Buyer can perform, and perhaps to verify the sale is an arm's length transaction vs. an insider deal that may not be in the best interest of the estate.

ENTER STAGE LEFT: PROBATE REFEREE
All estates are valued specifically for the "date of death" which is the date the decedent actually died. All estate valuations are intended to reflect values of the specific date of death. In nearly all probate cases, a Probate Referee is

appointed by the Court to provide an opinion of valuation for high-value assets. You won't have any say over who gets appointed. Like it or not, a Probate Referee is tasked with making sure that assets put in front of the Court are appropriately valued. "Appropriate valuation" does not necessarily reflect "accurate valuation," but we are talking about procedures of the Probate Court, not industry best practices. In many books about settling estates, the fact that there will be a Probate Referee is often not mentioned, or at best mentioned only in passing. However, it would be a mistake to assume that the actions taken by a Probate Referee don't matter and that you shouldn't pay attention, and even "get in front of" this step in the probate proceedings.

To be a Probate Referee, you must complete certain coursework and industry practice, be appointed by a judge and work as an officer of the court directly representing the presiding judge. If they have a background in real property, they will be asked to value real property; if they are expert in financial instruments and securities, they will be asked to value bonds and other negotiable instruments.

Valuing investments in stocks and mutual funds is relatively easy because there are historical records where the public can easily verify values of securities on specific dates.

After your initial filing with the Court to open probate, the Court will task one or more Probate Referees with the job of valuing the assets. Those referees are there to independently verify, prove and assess the value of the property that comes before the Court for distribution. The valuation such Referees will seek to determine is the "Date of Death" valuation, i.e., what were the specific assets worth at the time someone died. An estate may be settled months or years after death, which is why that date becomes important. Note that it doesn't matter how much someone paid for an asset prior to death, and whether they got a good deal or a bad deal. What matters is how much the assets were worth on the day they died.

If real property becomes part of a Probate Estate, the Probate Referee will be asked to do a "drive-by appraisal," which means that they will literally get in a car and drive by the property to make sure it's there. They may check assessed value online, and they may look at any other public assessment sites, such as Zillow, but they almost never get out of the car to inspect the property, and they almost never go inside. Why does that matter? The reason it matters is that Probate Referees are not required to use traditional real property valuation methods when valuing real property for the Probate Court. Real property value is defined as the present worth of future benefits arising from the ownership of the property. Unlike consumer goods that are quickly used, the benefits of real property are generally realized over a long period of time. Therefore, an estimate of a property's value must take into consideration economic and social trends, governmental controls or regulations and environmental conditions that may influence the four elements of value:

- Demand the desire or need for ownership supported by the financial means to satisfy the desire
- Utility: the ability to satisfy future owners' desires and needs
- Scarcity: the finite supply of competing properties
- Transferability: the ease with which ownership rights are transferred

Suppose a house you have inherited looks fabulous from the outside, but the decedent used the inside to cook crystal methamphetamine. The house may be completely uninhabitable, but the Probate Referee will report back to the Court that the house looks good, and is worth every penny of $500,000. That presents a problem when your real estate agent gets offers on the house, the highest of which comes in at $250,000. What then?

The general rule for Probate Court sales is that a judge will generally not approve a sale unless it is within 90% of the Probate Referee's valuation. On a house valued at $500,000, that means that a contract to purchase at anything less than $450,000 is likely to be immediately rejected by the Court. Anything above that 90% threshold, even if it's a lot higher, say $700,000, is no problem. The process in place to prove value is only concerned with making sure that assets aren't grossly undervalued.

If the estate you are tasked with administering includes real property, you will be well advised to hire experts to assess the physical condition of the home, apartment or commercial building *before* the Probate Court commences the Probate Referee valuation. Here is why I make this suggestion: If the property has not been maintained, and it has a lot of deferred maintenance, the Probate Referee will not have that knowledge and will not consider the cost to correct deferred maintenance in their valuation of the real property. I see this happen all the time. The result is, when you go to sell that real property, if the cost to cure the deferred maintenance results in low price purchase offers below the Court's valuation threshold, you will be forced to go to back to Court to seek approval to sell the property at a lower cost. This will result in substantial delays, you may lose your buyer, and have to start the whole process all over. It seriously sucks.

Here's how this can play out: In the case of a house with a high bid of $250,000 that is valued at $500,000 by the Probate Referee, the next step will be to petition the Court to have the property re-valued, which can be very cumbersome. Situations like this are common. Regardless of what the Probate Referee comes up with as a valuation number, you will either have to live with or work through it. Working through it can cost you a lot of time and potentially diminish the value of your property due to time burden to get the Court to "correct" the Probate Referee's valuation to reflect actual conditions of the property in relation to market conditions.

A smarter way to handle the value of real estate is to proactively hire a licensed appraiser or, a licesned real estate broker to provide a date of death value and a licensed contractor or property inspector to inspect the real property and issue appraisal or broker price opinion and structural reports. Include copies of the fee appraisal and property inspection reports as exhibits with your Inventory and Appraisal Court filing so that you'll have some evidence of the market value of the property that is closer to the actual value. Having that documentation from a qualified general contractor/property inspector and valuation from a licensed appraiser in place even before a Probate Referee is appointed by the Court, can address issues of the property's physical condition as well as current real estate market conditions before the Probate Referee values your property. A Referee will see the appraisal you've included with your filing, review the physical inspection report that details deferred maintenance or worse issues, and if he/she disagrees with the professional valuation number you have provided it will force the issue to the front. It is much better to resolve any issue of market value well before the assets are put on the market.

WHAT'S ALL THE STUFF WORTH?

Most of us manage to accrue mountains of stuff over the course of a lifetime - so much so that we are filling storage lockers at record rates! That pair of skis from 1959 might be a rare and valuable set made in France, or it could be worth zero. Who can tell? In Probate Court, most of the emphasis and focus will be on real estate and negotiable securities, not on furniture, clothes or bric-a-brac. And yet, some of that bric-a-brac might be valuable.

There are appraisal and estate liquidation services you can call that will estimate what personal property is worth, and will even help you sell it or auction it off. If you think you have something rare and valuable, you would generally take the item(s) to a pawn shop or experienced collector, and ask them to write up a valuation for the Court. While most people wouldn't think to ask a pawnbroker to estimate value, such people are usually good sources for determining an actual market value for coins, jewelry, musical instruments, furniture, collectibles and, they have excellent contacts with other experts to help with valuations too. They are a valuable resource.

In most cases, a Probate Court will not be keenly interested in the valuation of personal property, even though the entire estate will be subject to probate if there is no Living Trust. If you want to sell Aunt Martha's rare teacup collection to a friend for $10, even if it *might* be worth $1,000 to the right collector, a judge is extremely unlikely to intervene. Such matters are generally not relevant to the overall value of an estate. If it turns out that Aunt Martha was also a collector of Picasso drawings that she bought in Paris in 1937 when she was an art student, and the drawings are worth $10 Million, that will definitely be something the Court will want to know. While inheritance laws can change, as this is written there is a $10 Million federal tax-free threshold for most estates. For anything over and above that amount, Uncle Sam will want his share!

CREDITORS CLAIMS IN PROBATE

The process to Notice potential creditors in probate is more formal than in a trust estate, but it is a requirement of all estates, whether in probate or trusts. Trust estates are flexible by comparison. The Personal Representative in probate cases is required to complete and file with the court the Allowance or Rejection of Creditor's Claim - Form DE-174 for each creditor claim filed. Creditors will have 60 days to file a claim after receipt of the Notice is mailed, or four months after notice of Letters of Testamentary. Once a creditor claim is filed, the Personal Representative will have thirty days to pay, allow, or reject and contest the claim. The Probate Court has an established list of claims priority, and they are:

1. IRS or California Franchise Tax Board liens.
2. Administrative expenses - this includes paying your professional consultants!
3. Secured Creditors, e.g., a home loan secured by real property.
4. Funeral Expenses.
5. Family Allowance. A family allowance is a court-authorized payment(s) during probate to beneficiaries who were dependent upon the decedent for support.
6. Wage Claims.

7. General Debts, e.g., credit card bills take a low position on the totem pole of creditors.

STOCKS & BONDS

Like most people who are familiar with the probate system know, things don't happen quickly in Probate Court. In fact, the whole process moves incredibly slowly, with each cumbersome step required to be completed prior to the next cumbersome step. If you have assets of fluctuating value, do you need to be prepared to watch helplessly unless you have the express authority to act? No! As a Personal Representative or as a Trustee, you have a fiduciary obligation to protect and to preserve the value of the estate assets. If you are administering a probate, you cannot liquidate and distribute securities without court approval to distribute to heirs and beneficiaries, but you can, and you are expected to preserve the value of the portfolio, and that may mean you need to sell and buy different securities prior to final distribution to the beneficiaries. I recommend you consult with your attorney about preserving securities portfolios to determine if the local court has specific steps necessary to act at this level.

From the point at which you submit the petition to open probate, with a certified copy of a Death Certificate and an original Will, to the Probate Court, to the point when you receive a hearing and are given authority to administer an Estate, is often a two + month process - at best. Even if you are named in the Will as being the beneficiary of certain assets, you will not have authority to liquidate any assets until the Court gives you that express authority. The timeline to complete a probate case is typically nine to eighteen months. That should support my claim; there are a lot of necessary steps to complete the obligations of the Personal

Representative before he or she can petition the court to distribute to beneficiaries and close the probate case.

Where this often becomes a problem is in the case where A) there is no Living Trust, so you are subject to probate, and B) there are stocks in a brokerage account in the name of a decedent. If you are not named on the account, and you aren't given authority to sell securities in the account through Letters of Testamentary (which state that you are the Personal Representative of the Estate), you will have to sit on your hands as you watch the value of assets in the account bounce around until you have received the Letters of Testamentary. You will note on the California Probate Court's Letters of Testamentary form DE-150 that there are check boxes to indicate whether you, acting as the Administrator or Personal Representative, have Full Authority, Partial Authority or Blocked Authority to liquidate estate assets.

If you think that bad things will happen to the value of assets in an estate, and you have no authority to act, you could always Petition the Court to get permission to liquidate the assets and hold them in trust until final distribution is granted by the court. But consider that a noticed petition to the Court would be two months - and in some courts, is likely to be four months! Your attorney may try filing an ex parte petition if you seek the court's guidance for simple, uncontested matters, and/or there could be a loss of value to the estate if you do not act quickly.

A FEW IMPORTANT ASSETS NOT SUBJECT TO PROBATE

If there is a surviving spouse, and the decedent had a retirement account, those benefits will immediately go to the surviving spouse and not be subject to probate. Another example would be a Life Insurance policy with a named beneficiary, as Life Insurance policies naming individuals as beneficiaries are specifically excluded from probate. If the life insurance policy names the estate as the beneficiary, then it is subject to probate.

Any assets that are owned as "Joint Tenants with Rights of Survivorship" are also not subject to probate. If the assets are so named, the surviving member takes over the moment the joint tenant dies.

WHAT YOUR ATTORNEY WILL AND WILL NOT DO FOR YOU

The biggest mistake I see people make going into a probate process is to assume that their attorney will handle all the details. You should expect that your attorney will fill out the probate forms and file petitions and motions with the Court in proper sequence. Your attorney will be available to advise you on points of law until the Court approves all of your actions and approves distribution to beneficiaries. To close a probate estate in California, the Personal Representative must file a final account report and petition for final distribution, have the petition set for hearing, provide the required notice of the hearing to interested parties, e.g., heirs and beneficiaries, perhaps sometimes creditors too. Once you file the petition and proposed order to close the estate, the Clerk of the Court will give you a hearing date at the counter - often several months down the road. The petition for final distribution should give the court a detailed history of the probate case. The narrative should explain why the estate is ready to be closed, and how assets are to be distributed.

What your attorney will NOT do is:

- Give you any help with finding short-term money if you are tasked with administering an estate where the decedent had no cash. I am often asked to secure short-term private money loans to fund probate and trust estates, including those in litigation.
- Help you with any tax considerations, or help you with any tax questions/issues. They should have a recommendation for a good Certified Public Accountant to prepare the last income tax return for the decedent and the fiduciary tax return for the estate if you do not know one.
- Offer informed counsel on how to best position your real property and other high-value assets of the estate for protection and preservation. Do not assume attorneys understand real estate, construction, finance, or securities.
- Help you with taking an inventory of assets.
- Help you research and compile a list of potential creditors.
- Help you find important documents, e.g., title to the cars, timeshares/vacation rental interests owned by the decedent, locate insurance policies, etc.
- Change the name on utilities, insurance policies, and other accounts necessary to keep open in the name of the Personal Representative or Trustee during the probate case.
- Inform you that if you have real property that is not occupied, you must tell your insurance carrier the home or income property is vacant. If a property is vacant for over 30-days an insurance carrier may deny your claim if you did not tell them the property is vacant. That's a different type of coverage which must be specifically sought.
- Help you with an estate sale.

- Help you give away the personal property heirs and family members do not want - there is often a lot to go through if the decedent lived in the same place for decades prior to their death.
- Help you find professionals to perform maintenance on real property to protect and preserve it.
- Your probate attorney is not the one who gets calls from family members and beneficiaries who are in a tight spot and want to pressure you to "give them something" to tide them over.
- Your probate attorney is not the one takes the phone calls from the decedent's "friends" who make exaggerated claims they are owed money, or were promised the electric wheelchair uncle Sam used to get around in.

There is a lot more your probate attorney will not do, but I think you get the point I am making here; attorneys fill a narrow and critical role in the day to day tasks necessary for a Personal Representative or Trustee to administer an estate.

Attorneys in probate are typically paid by the hour, typically $375 per hour, but some charge as much as $700 or more. However, by legal statute, attorney's fees cannot exceed a certain percentage of the value of the estate (approximately 4% of the total value) and are subject to oversight by the Probate Court. In California, there are certain maximum percentages, and in most cases, attorneys will not charge the maximum. There is competition to handle probate cases, so you should know that attorneys will be willing to negotiate lower fee schedules if you have shopped around. As with all business transactions - caveat emptor!

CHAPTER SUMMARY:

- Probate is simply a process of 'proving up' the value of an estate.
- There is no "shortcut" in the 4-month period which creditors are allowed to file a claim against an estate or the 60-day period after they receive a Notice to Creditors from the estate administrator.
- Anticipate that a Probate Court will appoint a Probate Referee to establish the value of real property and submit your own valuation before that happens.
- Attorneys are essential to settling a probate estate, but they will primarily make sure that the forms and paperwork are filed correctly.
- Do not assume that your attorney will do anything except legal work.

5

Date of Death Valuations for Trust Estates

A surprisingly large number of estates I've worked on have all run into the same problem, so much so that I think that the problem needs to be highlighted: The Trustee of an estate has simply failed to pay attention to getting valuations of assets at the time of death. In probate, the Court will always appoint a Probate Referee to value estate assets. Trust estate administration does not have Court oversight like probate estates do, so you have to do this on your own. And if you miss this step, it will cause you a world of problems when you try to settle the estate and file the final fiduciary tax return.

It always seems to happen the same way. At some point, the Trustee suddenly realizes that valuations are needed of assets including real property, securities, jewelry, coins, art, vehicles, travel trailers, tools and other valuables you may have already sold or given away. Oh, and by the way, did we mention that we don't want the valuation as of today, we need the valuation at the time of death. Oops.

For certain kinds of assets, securities mostly, getting a date of death valuation is relatively easy – just look at the financial statement. All the other assets, however, are genuinely problematic. How do you value a house at a specific date that may be years in the past? What comps do you use? How do you decide what condition the house was in? I am often asked to produce Broker Opinion of Values for homes or income property long after the date of death – often years afterward. It is painstaking work to produce defendable valuations for property values that need to be dated years earlier.

Income tax advisors, CPA's and financial planners, understand an estate's requirement that a Personal Representative or, a Trustee, is required to obtain date of death valuations for real property, but sometimes that information is not communicated properly or with sufficient urgency. There often seems to be no rush in getting things appraised since, after all, the prior owner has died, right? And probate matters move at glacial speed, so getting values is often forgotten, overlooked or just ignored until someone asks for them. But not current valuations, of course, they must be date of death valuations.

An estate is required to inventory personal and real property assets to establish the value for the date which the decedent died; it is a called a "date of death valuation." If you do not tackle the date of death valuations soon after the settlor of a trust dies, the valuations become increasingly more difficult as time passes. I need to keep repeating this because so many people don't seem to fully appreciate what it means!

Estates that are subject to probate are automatically referred to a court-appointed "Probate Referee" who is appointed by the court to inventory and value all personal and real property assets of an estate. I also mention this often in this book because Probate Referee "appraisals" are notoriously poor quality and because they are not required to employ professional standards of valuation.

I have seen many situations when the first spouse dies, the surviving spouse and family carry on with their lives and fail to probate the estate of the decedent. That is not a problem if the person who dies does not have real property or other significant assets totaling more than $150,000 or if the real property is owned as joint tenants with right of survivorship. However, when a person who owns real property that is not titled as joint tenancy with right of survivorship, and the surviving spouse and family fail to probate and settle the estate, you will likely find yourself having to petition for probate of the first spouse who died before you can sell or finance the real property that he/she had title to prior to death.

As I write this, I am consulting on a litigation matter where we must probate a 25-year old estate before the recently deceased surviving spouse's estate can be settled. This is not uncommon. How do you satisfy the date of death valuation of an estate when it is decades old? It is a conundrum, and it happens more often than you might expect.

TAX ISSUES AND DATE OF DEATH
Some of the best advice I will give you is to seek out an experienced tax professional that has extensive experience

in filing fiduciary tax returns. Not all Certified Professional Accountants (CPA's) have the qualifications or, experience in filing fiduciary and estate tax returns. Tax considerations in probate and trust matters often do not get addressed early enough to effectively strategize tax mitigation measures while settling estates. As a result, you may be surprised to find beneficiaries having tax consequences. Today, estates are not taxed unless they are worth many millions of dollars, so people may assume there will be no tax owed upon the distribution of assets to beneficiaries. But that assumption will not apply if an asset was valued at $100,000 at the date of death but is sold out of probate or in a trust for $120,000. That scenario would be considered a gain, and therefore the beneficiaries may find they have a taxable event.

To avoid unnecessary taxes inuring to beneficiaries, consult with a qualified tax or financial consultant before liquidating assets. Again, Probate Referee valuations may not be accurate values, so I encourage you to still obtain fee appraisals from professionally qualified appraisers. Not doing so can result in significant tax obligations to beneficiaries that may have otherwise been avoided if the assets had been accurately valued.

Oftentimes, trustees do not make appointments to meet with CPA's or financial consultants until they have liquidated estate assets and they are ready to file the final fiduciary tax return. Note that in most cases it will probably take well over a year from the date of death before the personal representative (PR) or trustee is prepared to file the estate's final return with the internal revenue service. If the estate owns real property, and the real estate market is appreciating, you may well realize a gain in value above what the asset was worth at the time of death. Conversely, if market values are declining, you may realize a loss of value at the time of sale, and the estate may realize a loss, which also inures to the beneficiaries and can be used to offset future taxes.

If you tackle the inventory and valuation of assets early, your duties as a PR or trustee will be a lot easier. Obtaining appraisals early in the process results in more accurate valuations. So, my advice, whether a probate or trust situation, is to get all your appraisals done right away and file them away.

Probate estates are required to provide an inventory to the Probate Referee who will value the probated property of the decedent. The Probate Referee will value real property, securities, and personal property. Trust estates are different; you will not have the court overseeing your administration unless you are in litigation. You may expect probate and trust attorneys will advise you or remind you to complete the trust asset valuations, but they rarely do because taxation is not an area they typically specialize in, so it is not a "top of mind" consideration for attorneys.

Probate referee appraisals are notoriously poor quality, and I strongly recommend that personal representatives obtain fee appraisals, or employ licensed real estate brokers to prepare detailed Broker Opinion of Value to submit with the petition to open probate. One very good reason to obtain fee appraisals, especially for real property, is because when beneficiaries inherit, they inherit the property at the date of death valuation as their tax basis value for the asset. This is what in real estate we refer to as inheriting at the "stepped up basis valuation" which means your inherited value basis will likely be higher than the decedents' value basis when they died.

Real property investors who own income producing properties for a long period of time depreciate them on their annual tax returns. The depreciation, over time, reduces the decedent's tax basis valuation. The phrase "I cannot afford to sell because my taxable event would take all my appreciation" is based upon fact; long-term real property owners "tax basis" valuation basis sometimes becomes so low, that if they were to sell a real property asset, every dollar of the sale price, over the tax basis amount, is taxed at favorable capital gains tax rate for federal taxes.

Note, however, that the depreciation that investor took over the preceding years of ownership is "recaptured," the amount that was depreciated over the holding period is taxed as ordinary income! Add state taxes to the two applied federal tax brackets, and you end with little to show for yourself. This is why real property is so commonly left to beneficiaries because the person who worked hard and made good investments in real property literally couldn't afford to sell their property and live off the equity.

CHAPTER SUMMARY:
- Get valuations of all assets as soon as possible after someone has died, even if you don't immediately file a probate.
- There are many great reasons for getting date of death valuations, the most compelling of which is that it will help you to avoid taxes and achieve maximum gain on the ultimate sale of those assets.
- Consult with qualified tax and legal professionals on all valuation, tax and appraisal issues. Doing so will save you many headaches and heartaches down the road.

6

Legal Counsel in Trust and Probate Estates

I f you want to administer your probate without using an attorney, you can use some of the books, such as <u>Nolo's How to Probate an Estate</u>, <u>The Executor's Handbook</u> and <u>Estate & Trust Administration for Dummies</u>. If the estate you plan to administer has assets under $150,000, such resources are likely to be useful. Your job won't be easy, but if you are reasonably diligent and are willing to sift through the details, those books will certainly be good resources. At $150,000 or less, your probate matter can be handled in an expedited and simplified manner called the Small Estate Procedure. Estates over $150,000 in assets, however, are considerably more complex and cumbersome to administer, because they don't qualify for the Small Estate Procedure.

Either way, before you decide that you want to handle the case yourself (known in the business as 'In Pro Per' which is a Latin term that essentially means acting on your own behalf), you should consider that even something as simple as filing a document can consume hours of your day and likely multiple trips to the Clerk of the Probate Court. Some Courts require that holes be punched in the document in a certain place, or that documents be stapled together, or that documents should never be stapled together! Failure to follow court procedures to the absolute letter of the local court will likely result in your documents being rejected by the Clerk of the Court. You could easily find yourself making three or four trips to the Clerk before you'll have the documents prepared to their satisfaction and acceptance. I personally have had the Clerk accept a filing only to be called by the clerk's office later in the day or the following day, telling me the Probate Examiner has rejected my filing on some legal or procedural basis, but they won't tell you any details because they cannot give you legal advice. If you decide to handle the probate yourself, without legal counsel, be prepared to develop the patience of Job, or you may pop a blood vessel!

WHAT IS A PROBATE EXAMINER?

A Probate Examiner is usually an attorney who works for the Probate Court. Their job is to review all probate documents for content and legal requirements before they are reviewed by the court. The examiner's role is to make sure the probate petition is complete and contains all required information according to the law. If you attend Probate Court hearings, you will note the Probate Examiner often sits to the side of the Judge, and the court confers with the examiner during the hearing.

The Probate Examiner will make notes when reviewing probate petitions or motions. These are referred to as Probate Examiner Notes. Most California counties that I have personally worked in have Probate Court websites where you can access the Probate Examiner Notes using your case number. Attorney's regularly look up the examiner notes before showing up to the hearing so they can properly prepare to address any concerns of the examiner before showing up to the hearing.

If you don't consider your time especially valuable, or if you don't have anything better to do, acting 'In Pro Per' for a probate matter may be just the hobby you were looking for. In the vast majority of cases, however, and certainly for those over $150,000 in assets but even those below that threshold, paying in the range of $3,000-5,000 for legal representation to execute all these steps, is a very good investment. And remember that by law, as a Trustee or Personal Representative, you have the right, and are expected to use the services of qualified professionals, and pay for those services out of the assets of the estate.

HOW TO FIND AND HIRE A COMPETENT LEGAL COUNSEL

As someone who has decades of experience in and around Probate Courts, I have seen very few situations go well when a Personal Representative or Trustee decides to go 'In Pro Per.' It hardly ever works out as expected. The rules of the game are too complex, and the learning curve is too steep. You can read all the books out there, but you will still probably miss opportunities to maximize the return on assets for the estate. Hiring an attorney to represent you in a trust or probate matter is always a good choice. Let me repeat: It is *always* a good idea to have a competent lawyer in your corner. Many people pick up a

"Probate For Dummies" book and try to do it themselves. Yes, especially when you decide to go it alone,
there is a reason why such books may be aptly named!

The first couple of times that I had to personally administer
an estate, I really felt lost, and didn't understand a lot of
basic elements of estate settlement, even though I had significant experience being a Court Appointed Receiver I
was floundering in the probate process, and again later
when I acted as a trustee for the first time. I certainly knew
a lot more than the average person going to Probate Court
for the first time, but still, I had no direct experience and
came to realize I was flying blind much of the time, and it
turned out to be a lot more work than I expected.

My lack of experience in this world caused me to have
enormous stress at various times. For example, I thought
there were time limitations on filing certain documents,
and that there was a deadline by which time I had to settle
the estate. My attorney never told me that there were no
real deadlines! In fact, I learned much later that you could
keep an estate open for years; indeed, I'm currently administering an estate that I've been working to get closed for
nearly three years, and that is not considered long by estate
standards. Doing things right is paramount in estate issues,
whereas doing it fast is usually not that important. Sometimes it just takes a long time to liquidate assets, especially
if they need to be positioned or reposition to maximum
benefit.

Even though it is always the right choice to hire a lawyer,
finding the right attorney to help guide you through a probate or trust estate case may be one of your biggest challenges. Start with the fact that most people don't know a
probate or trust estates attorney, and the fact that very

often an attorney needs to be found during a time of grief and high stress, and it is no wonder that many people report that they "made the wrong choice" when they think back upon their experience.

Before I explain how you should go about finding a good attorney, let me arm you with a few facts:

- There is a statutory scale of charges that attorneys are allowed to charge in probate cases.
- It's a graduated scale:
  - 4% of the first $100,000 of the gross value of the probate estate.
  - 3% of the next $100,000.
  - 2% of the next $800,000.
  - 1% of the next $9 million.
  - 0.5% of the next $15 million.

What this means is that no matter who you pick, in most cases there will be a limit on how much an attorney can charge.

Attorney fees are always negotiable! As with most business transactions, the market for legal services is based on market forces. There are lots and lots of probate attorneys, which means that most attorneys are quite willing to discuss different payment arrangements. Do not be dissuaded by oak paneling and plush carpeting. Someone may hand you an impressive document that looks like it was etched in stone, but rates, fees, and charges are fluid. If you are price conscious, you can negotiate fees for legal representation.

Before you start interviewing attorneys, you need to do some thinking about what kind of case you have, and what kind of attorney you should be looking for. You need to have some basic idea of what services you are likely to need. You may be thinking, how the heck am I supposed to know that? I have never done this before. If you suspect "undue influence" or wrongdoing by others, you may potentially end up in a fight. There may be a necessity to file a lawsuit and hire a litigator - someone who will go into court argue your case for you. Perhaps one of the beneficiaries was taking things from the deceased prior to death, then what you're looking for in legal representation is different than someone who would simply be helping you to file the correct forms at the correct time. If you think you'll need an attorney for more than just the statutory requirements for filings, then you want to find someone who is qualified to effectively fight in the Probate Court, and when appropriate, in civil court.

In the world of attorneys who specialize in administering probate estates, it's generally an old guard. The attorneys you'll mostly find will do everything slowly, and they tend to be very passive - at least that's been my experience over the past several decades. You'll want to work with someone who is compatible with your personality because if you're a Type A personality (like me) who likes to go through your list and check off boxes, you might not work well with many probate attorneys because they are never in a hurry. People are dead, so there is rarely a situation where time is of the essence -- unless you have a situation where undue influence or elder financial abuse appears to have occurred. There are clear-cut differences between attorneys who will administer the legal points and work through the issues of settling an estate, and someone who will act as an advocate to take action and file a well-crafted lawsuit on your behalf if that becomes necessary to protect beneficiaries.

Let's assume, for this chapter, that all you need is to find an attorney who can help you complete the required statutory paperwork for probate, and that you don't need a litigator. Should you shop for an attorney based purely on price? Isn't it better to hire someone at $300 per hour instead of $700 per hour if they'd be doing the same thing? As in most things, it's not that simple. If you anticipate that your case is even a little complicated - for example, you might assume you'll need to do 'clawbacks' to get monies returned to the estate that should not have been paid or taken by others not authorized to do so, you will need an attorney who has experience doing that, as well as an attorney who is a skilled negotiator. Especially in cases where you believe that 'undue influence' or elder financial abuse has occurred, you would almost never want to shop for an attorney on the basis of cost. In such cases, you will want to find the most skillful and experienced practitioner you can find.

SHOPPING FOR AN ATTORNEY

A few of the first steps you should take when you are searching for a lawyer are:

- Review all the information you can find online: What certifications or accreditations do they have? Can you find peer reviews? In many ways, this is no different from the way you assess any other scope of services for a professional, be it a dentist, doctor or accountant.
- If you know people who have recently lost loved ones, you might reach out to them and ask who represented them. I would always consider asking

friends and relatives, especially because attorneys often travel in certain circles and will want to keep their reputation strong within a group that is a good referral source.

- If you know any other attorneys, but they don't practice in probate or estate work, you should definitely reach out to ask for a recommendation or two. When you talk with an attorney, try to be as specific about the kind of attorney you think would match up well with you. Do you need a tenacious bulldog? Do you want someone who is younger and more eager? Do you want someone who is a nice person and isn't too gung-ho? How you envision that person will help you narrow the search.

- Your State Bar Association will also be a good source of referrals. Every State Bar has a website specifically set up for this purpose, and if none of the above methods have worked, this is certainly a better option than looking on Yelp or Craigslist!

- You may have the choice as to whether you want to hire your attorney on an hourly basis, perhaps with a cap on the total amount you will spend, or whether you want an attorney to take the case on a contingency basis.

  o If you have limited financial resources and cannot afford to pay a retainer and hourly fees, you should certainly consider a contingency. Even in such cases, there will be a limit on how much an attorney can charge. You will likely end up paying more through a contingency agreement, but your out of pocket expenses will be avoided or mitigated. If you are a beneficiary who has been wrongfully excluded from an estate, and you are sitting with nothing today, the art of the

> possible in contingency representation is that you could end up with 60-75% of something, which is a lot better than what you started with. Right?

After you've settled on a list of potential attorneys, preferably three or four, you'll need to set up face-to-face consultations with each one. Don't take the easy route and do it just by phone. Your consult need not be more than 15 or 20 minutes, but at that time both you and the attorney will know whether it's a good match. Do you have a rapport? Do you feel comfortable discussing private family matters with him or her? Do you get a sense of competence and integrity? If you only speak with one attorney, you'll have no frame of reference. Maybe the first one you meet will be the best; after you meet two or three more you'll be better prepared to make that decision.

Make no mistake - the interview will work both ways. Yes, you are the client, and you want to choose the best-qualified person for the job, but the best attorneys are in high demand, and they will be interviewing you as well. Do you seem like a high maintenance client? Are you likely to eat up a lot of their time with unimportant requests? Are your expectations unrealistic? Don't be surprised if an attorney you want decides that your case "isn't a good fit" for his or her practice.

I was fired by an estate attorney one time. Seriously, I met with this guy immediately after my mother passed away with my two sisters. I was already the successor trustee of our mother's estate. This attorney was a friend of my older sister, and he did a lot of probate law, he also prepared my sister and her husband's living trust. I remember when we met at his office, he instructed us that there is no rush to get through the administration of the trust estate. A few days after our first consultation, I signed the engagement paperwork; I paid the attorney a retainer fee. When I returned home after my mother's memorial service, I wrote this attorney an email asking him to provide me with a bullet list of things I will need to do in order to finalize the trust estate of my mother. My email message to this attorney I just hired stated he can work at his pace and I can work at my pace, to complete the necessary steps to finalize the estate and the trust distributions to my siblings, I was anxious to get "my list" and race through it. He wrote me back saying he received my message and he will respond shortly. Two days later I received a piece of mail from this attorney's office; inside the envelope was a check in the amount of the retainer payment I had made to him with a letter saying he was not interested in working with me!

Because you may well be in a state of shock or may be grieving, you may not be in the best frame of mind to interview attorneys and make the difficult choice needed. If possible, consider bringing a friend or relative with you to the first meeting for both support and advice. You'll want to find somebody who you are compatible with because, once they are hired, you will have both time and money invested in keeping the relationship strong.

What do you need to ask each attorney in that initial consultation? Here is a short list:

- What steps do you expect to take over the course of the engagement?
- What is the expected timing?
- What will the attorney do (specifically) and what will the attorney not do?

- What problems do they see happen that could easily be avoided?
- What kinds of unexpected expenses or issues should be anticipated?

In wrapping up the affairs of someone's life, especially someone you were close to such as a family member or a parent, you want someone who you'll feel comfortable with. You should also keep in mind, however, that you probably won't have that much interaction with your attorney once the case starts. You won't be making two trips each week to sit down and chat! Attorneys are required to file, over the course of the probate, perhaps a half dozen form petitions to settle the estate. For them, those are just benchmarks. But if you are the administrator or personal representative of an estate, the work between those benchmarks will mostly be handled by you - not your attorney.

A LITIGATOR VERSUS A TRUST/PROBATE LITIGATOR

In most cases, you will not need a litigator, but if you do need a litigator in a trust or probate estate matter, there is a big difference between a general litigator and a probate litigator. Trust and probate litigation is a highly specialized area, and there are steps in the probate code that lots of litigators who do not specialize in trust and probate litigation are not familiar with. The difference between litigation in State Court and Probate Court and general litigation is large. An attorney, no matter how well qualified, but who has no experience litigating trust or probate matters, is not someone you want to represent you in Probate Court over a legal complaint. In cases of undue influence or elder financial abuse, it is critically important to find an attorney who has litigated such matters in probate and civil courts. New laws are being passed all the time regarding undue influence and elder financial abuse. There may be a strategic advantage to filing elder financial abuse cases in civil court over Probate Court due to the way preponderance of evidence is considered in the respective courts.

Let me give you a common example of why this is important. Imagine a situation involving a deceased married couple who had both been previously married and had separate families. Each spouse has a Living Trust because they had separate families. The husband often dies before his wife, and the wife is tasked with administering his Trust. Because she is elderly and in poor health, she may not be able to handle her husband's estate administration matters very well. Distributions are not made, and beneficiaries to her husband's estate get frustrated and hire an attorney, a good, solid litigator, to sue the wife because she is not fulfilling her duties as the Trustee.

I remember one case well, where if the attorney who filed the action against the surviving spouse in a similar situation had known what he was doing in Probate Court, he would have immediately requested that the Court substitute in a new, professional Trustee who was competent and capable of handling the estate and making the distributions. This is, in fact, a fairly routine matter that is handled efficiently by most Probate Courts. It should have been a case closed. Instead, the case I am recalling the litigator's lawsuit ended up becoming protracted, and more litigation ensued when the surviving spouse died during the litigation. That case dragged on for more than three years all because, in my opinion, some beneficiaries hired an otherwise competent litigator who had inadequate experience in probate matters. The underlying issue in that three-year legal battle might have been settled inside of 90 to 120 days if the litigator knew to petition the Court for a substitute trustee.

IF YOU'RE NOT THE EXECUTOR, PERSONAL REPRE-SENTATIVE OR TRUSTEE, DO YOU NEED AN ATTOR-NEY?

If you weren't named by will or Trust document as an Executor, Personal Representative or Trustee, does it make sense to hire your own attorney? In most cases, the answer is no. Heirs and estate beneficiaries don't need an attorney unless you believe that you are not being treated fairly, and you can't work through the issue(s) equitably with whoever was charged with settling the estate. If you can't find common ground, or if you believe you aren't going to get a fair deal, then hiring a plaintiff's lawyer to put the problem in front of a Probate Judge will be your best option. In that case, you definitely will need an attorney who may petition the Court to appoint you as a co-Executor, co-Trustee or co-Personal Representative or to substitute in a professional fiduciary to settle the estate properly and equitably.

It is common practice to have more than one Executor, Trustee or Personal Representative, but a Probate Court will have to approve the arrangement. As a practical matter, however, it does make things more complicated. I have previously served as a co-Trustee, and currently serve as a co-Trustee, and can tell you that it's a lot more work for everyone because you'll be serving by committee. No decisions will be made until an agreement is reached between the named Executors, Trustees or Personal Representatives, which means that every issue is likely to be debated. If you are OK with that and know what you are getting into, you will still need an attorney to convince a judge that your appointment as co-administrator is important to the successful closure of the case.

The time to address who the decedent named in their will to act as the Executor or Trustee is usually at the very start of the proceedings. If there is no will or living trust, then the Court will appoint an Administrator to act as the Personal Representative. Once a Probate Court has issued Letters of Testamentary, it becomes harder, and ultimately more expensive, to substitute someone else as Personal Representative or Trustee of the estate. It can be done, of course, especially if it can be shown that the person who was appointed isn't qualified or isn't doing the job well. Any objection will have to be based on cause. Keep in mind that if you want to get someone replaced, it's not guaranteed that the Court will appoint you either to take over or co-manage. More than likely, a Probate Court will appoint a professional fiduciary to substitute in and administer the estate because they have the experience to carry out the responsibilities.

If someone isn't doing a good job in settling an estate, I would strongly advise that an attorney is hired to petition the court to substitute in a qualified replacement to act as the Personal Representative or Trustee. Trustees and Personal Representatives who don't know what they're doing can cause enormous financial damage, and once the damage is done it often can't be undone.

Where there is known wrongdoing by either the Personal Representative or beneficiaries, you will absolutely need an attorney to represent you in Probate Court, even though there is no guarantee of a favorable outcome.

A WORD OF CAUTION: MAKING SURE ATTORNEY FEES DON'T CONSUME THE ESTATE

Let me tell you a brief story that explains what can happen when you have multiple Trustees representing an estate. In this situation, there was litigation going on with a Trust, but the beneficiaries ended up settling the litigation during mediation. A settlement agreement was drafted and signed by all the parties. That should have been the end of the story, but it was actually just the start.

As it turned out, the estate litigation settlement agreement was subject to pre-existing decedent litigation that had actually started two years earlier, prior to the settlor trustee's death. If someone who dies is involved in litigation at the time of their death, that litigation doesn't just "go away." The heirs and beneficiaries of the decedent's estate will be passed the baton to continue the litigation until is settled or adjudicated.

The cost of hiring attorneys to fight over probate and estate assets should always be weighed against the net potential benefit. Before taking the plunge to correct what may indeed be malfeasance or fraud, it is always prudent to consider the ultimate cost in relation to the value of the estate. You may win the case but find yourself owing thousands of dollars in legal fees - a true pyrrhic victory if ever there is one.

CHAPTER SUMMARY:

- Hiring a good attorney will be the smartest decision you can make.
- Shop around for an attorney who fits your needs and personality.
- Attorneys are incredibly useful, but their services should be used appropriately. Asking an attorney to go above and beyond will often generate huge legal fees.
- A good attorney will be able to advise you when and what to fight, and when to walk away.

7

Proving the Will in Probate Court

Why probate? At its core, probate really has only three functions:

1. Deciding if a will is valid or, if no will exists, the Court will appoint an Administrator to administer the probate as an intestate estate.
2. Identifying and resolving all outstanding financial obligations of the decedent.
3. Distributing the remainder of the estate assets to court-approved heirs and/or beneficiaries.

All the rules, regulations and procedures that allow a probate case to be resolved are there in support of those simple functions. Trust estates focus only on item numbers 2 and 3 above, because a living trust, which becomes irrevocable upon the death of the Settlor Trustee (person or people who created the living trust), will not require court supervision administering the estate.

There's not usually much drama in Probate Court because there are seldom life and death decisions being made. Just the opposite! A death has already occurred, and now it's up to the Court to clean up and resolve any issues relating to that person's financial affairs, property and heirs/beneficiaries. Even if there isn't much drama, the stakes can still be extremely high. Probate Courts transfer many billions of dollars in assets, and arguments over those assets can, and do sometimes, go on for years.

In probate cases, an executor (if there is a will) or an administrator (if there is no will) is appointed by the Court as personal representative to collect assets, pay debts and expenses, and then distribute the remainder of the decedent's estate to the beneficiaries (those who have the legal right to inherit), all under the supervision of the Court.

Probate cases usually take 9 to 18 months, but some probate cases take years before they can be settled if the decedent's estate has a lot of issues or, if it is contested. This is all in support of the main purpose of probate, which is to prove up the assets, prove up the debts and prove up the distributions of property and assets to the rightful heirs.

PROBATE ESTATES WITH LESS THAN $150,000 IN ASSETS

If the properties and assets of the decedent are worth less than $150,000, you can use what I call "short form probate," but which is known in California as Form DE-310. Short form probate is relatively quick because it has fewer steps than a regular probate filing, but the $150,000 limit is hard and fast. Even if an estate has, for example, $200,000 in assets but also $150,000 in debts, you won't be able to file the short form because, by California Probate Rules, the Court looks at total asset values of the decedent, not net asset values. The Court does not take into consideration any of the debts when determining the size of the estate. If you are lucky, and you are able to file a short form probate, you may be able to get through the entire process in a little as 40-50 days.

However, note that if there is any real property (land, houses, etc.) in the estate, even if it is worth less than $150,000, you won't be able to use the short form process. The reason is that petitions to transfer real property title must go through probate. There will also be a requirement for valuation of any real property, and this is where a Probate Referee will be a requirement.

PROBATE ESTATES WITH MORE THAN $150,000 IN ASSETS

By law, if an estate has more than $150,000 in assets, (unless all the assets are protected by a Trust) you must go to Probate Court, and you must open a probate case. Start to finish, the least amount of time a probate will take is nine months, and it is fairly common to see cases go on for 18 months. In some rare cases involving significant assets with major disputes, probate cases can literally drag on for years, or even decades!

Whoever has possession of the will is called "The Custodian." Within 30 days of the date of death, the custodian must take the original will, file it with the Probate Clerk, and send a copy of the will to the executor, if an executor can be found, and to any beneficiaries named in the will. If a custodian does not do these things, he or she can be sued for damages caused to the estate.

Someone called "The Petitioner" must then start the court filing to open a probate case. The petitioner is usually going to be someone who will be nominated, either by the decedent in their Will or by the court when intestate, to administer the estate. Filings are generally done in one of three ways:

- Petition for Probate of Will and for Letters of Testamentary
- Petition for Probate of Will and for Letters of Administration with Will Annexed. This means that you would be filing for your letters of administration with a will attached that has specific codicils attached to it.
- Petition for Letters of Administration (if there is no will - a so-called 'intestate' filing.)

After you file with the court, a Probate Clerk will set a hearing date and will accept all of your probate documents. Note that a clerk's acceptance does not mean that the court accepts them. Once the documents are filed, a Probate Examiner will review all the documents' content and will decide if they meet or comply with the court requirements and the law for filing.

The next step will be to send a notice of the hearing date to anyone who may have rights to get some part of the estate, such as surviving family members or any other person named in the will. An important point to keep in mind is that a petitioner in Probate Court cannot mail these notices directly. *They must be sent by a third party who is not part of the case.* Also, while it sounds very old-fashioned (and it is) you will also need to publish a notice in a newspaper of general circulation. A newspaper notice is actually an important step. There are papers in circulation specifically for required legal filings, and the only people who read them are usually people who use them as lead generation for new business. Even though the newspaper notice requirement for probate cases has probably outlived its usefulness, this archaic practice is unlikely to change anytime soon.

After all the paperwork has been filed, and proper notices have been given, a judge will decide who to appoint to be in charge as the personal representative of the estate (also known as the "administrator" or "executor" - the names are interchangeable, although there are distinctions based on whether there is a will, and if someone is specifically named.) The first job of the personal representative is to gather all the assets and prepare an inventory for the court (in California it's Form DE-160). The Court may, in some cases, also need to appoint a Probate Referee to establish values for all the nonmonetary assets of the estate.

After that, the steps in California Probate Court are usually done in this order:

- Filing of a Formal Notice of Administration to Creditors (Form DE-157), and the payment of any outstanding debts.
- Filing of a tax return for the person who died. The estate itself will get a new Tax ID number and will need to file tax returns until the estate is finally settled and closed. One notable detail should be covered here; the calendar year of death you should expect to have to file a personal tax return as well as a fiduciary tax return, be sure to discuss this with your tax professional.

- Decisions by the Probate Court about who gets what property.
- A Report of Sale and Petition for Order Confirming Sale of Real Property (Form DE-260). As noted earlier, this form will be required even if the real property is worth $1,000 or less.
- A final report to the court by the Personal Representative which provides a final plan and accounting.
- After the court receives receipts showing that everyone received their property from the estate, the court will discharge the personal representative and officially close the case.

Note that each one of these steps can require significant time, knowledge and resources. Having an experienced attorney in your corner will prove to be an important advantage. Too many things can go wrong and cause both emotional and financial distress, so I strongly suggest that you never go it alone.

ASSETS THAT ARE NOT SUBJECT TO PROBATE

A quick note about the kinds of assets that won't need to be going through probate. If you have an attorney, he or she will likely give you more specific guidance, but this list will at least give you an idea of what is and is not likely to be of importance. Keep in mind that even though lots of assets are excluded, it is often necessary for a survivor to take legal steps to clarify their position of ownership of transferred or distributed property.

Here is a quick list of assets that are generally not subject to probate:

- Any assets held in joint names with rights of survivorship, which might include bank accounts owned by multiple people including the deceased.
- Community property (usually husband and wife) with rights of survivorship.
- Contracts - most commonly life insurance policies with a named beneficiary. (However, if the estate itself is the beneficiary, then it is subject to probate.)
- Cars, boats and mobile homes.
- Property held in trust - especially a living trust.

WHY IS PROBATE SO HARD?!

All of the above information is fairly straightforward, and from the outside, it would seem that anyone with a reasonable amount of intelligence and persistence should be able to navigate the process without that much difficulty. Probate looks deceptively simple, but the subtle complexities can be maddening and frustrating.

Where difficulties usually arise is when there is any sort of disagreement. As soon as someone objects, the court must stop to examine the reasons for disagreement and figure out how to resolve it. Sometimes people lay claim to assets that aren't rightfully theirs. Sometimes claims of undue influence or elder financial abuse are raised. Sometimes someone makes a procedural mistake, such as transferring assets that weren't theirs or incorrectly sending out notices, and the process grinds to a halt.

Remember that you may be in a hurry to get title or possession of certain assets, but the court is never going to be in a hurry. If you can ratchet down your expectations of a quick resolution, you will find the probate process less stressful.

One other difficulty I see all the time with probate cases is that the heirs are strapped for cash, and can't even muster up enough money to hire a good attorney or some of the other professionals who might maximize their return on assets. Something to consider, in such cases, is for the estate to take out what is known as a 'hard money loan,' which is a cash loan against assets where the interest rate is usually high - often 9% to 11.5%, plus about 3 points to the lender up front as a 'loan fee'.

The advantage of hard money loans is that they provide immediate liquidity to heirs and beneficiaries so that professionals can be hired to work on the probate case. Such loans are not personally guaranteed if they are for business purposes and not personal purposes, so there are no credit checks; the lender will have a lien against assets (usually real property) for which they will be paid in full once the estate is settled or, the property is sold. The downside, of course, is that they are expensive. If you don't need immediate cash, I would advise most people to avoid hard money loans if you can. But if all else fails, this is a viable and potentially useful tool. It is also one of the most frequent tasks I am asked to perform; finding a private money lender to fund an estate that has no cash.

If you need to find a hard money lender, ask a real estate broker for a reference, or carefully search for private money lenders online. If you are in California, I have a website dedicated to helping people find good private money lenders to fund their estates. The website address is https://integrityestatelending.org/. As with all things financial, you need to do your homework and tread carefully, or you may put yourself, or the estate, in a poor position.

CHAPTER SUMMARY:

- If you are tasked with managing a probate estate with less than $150,000 in assets, you should take advantage of the short form process.
- The steps in probate are all essential and must be done both correctly and in the correct order. It is usually best to have an attorney guide you through the maze of forms and hearings.
- If the estate is cash poor, there are ways to raise cash that will help to maximize the ultimate return on assets.

8

Understanding and Complying
With Probate Court Procedures

I n recent decades, attorneys, bankers, and professional fiduciaries were typically the ones in charge of probating estates. The trend these days, however, is that more and more civilians, people with no training and no background in probate, are being tasked with being personal representatives. Surprisingly, many people with enormous net worth, lots of assets, and access to the best financial professionals often don't take even modest steps to protect their assets for their heirs and descendants. Who wants to write a will? Who wants to think about their own death, and what will happen to their property after they die? It's a depressing thought, which makes it likely to be put off.

Because so many novices are now being thrust into managing estates, the likelihood of errors and poor execution is now incredibly common. People may buy all the requisite books, but even at the most basic level, there are important steps that most inexperienced personal representatives and trustees trip up on. Let's cover some of those steps and procedures:

You probably know that you need to have a Probate Court's letters of testamentary in hand prior to formally gathering assets and tallying up true creditor obligations of the estate. As a practical matter, however, you will usually be better off not waiting for those letters *before* you start your informal survey of assets and creditor accounting.

If you think about it, it's really a 'chicken and egg problem,' but with a real solution. As an undergraduate at Cal, my first real estate development course was with a professor whose family business had built tens of thousands of homes. He frequently referred to 'chicken and egg' situations, which was his way of looking at problems. That framework has stuck with me all these years later because it still helps me to think through how to prioritize plans and procedures.

In this case, the assets and liabilities of the estate are the 'eggs' you want to protect and hatch, and the letters of testamentary powers are the 'chickens' you ultimately hope to have. To extend the analogy, you can't start counting those chickens until the court gives you authority, but you do need to keep the eggs warm in the meantime!

What that means is that as early as possible, you will want to gather the decedent's assets, and start assessing what the decedent's debts and other financial obligations. You'll want to protect the assets from conversion and commingling by others. Note that at the same time, from the

Probate Court's eyes, you don't really have standing to do that until you have filed the probate petition, you have filed the will, you get a hearing date, you go before the judge, and the court authorizes you to be the Personal Representative or Executor named in the will. At that moment you will have legal standing, but not a minute before.

My recommendation is to do everything you can to protect assets of the estate as soon as you can, with or without the letters of testamentary in hand. Why? The simple reason is that when people die, their possessions and assets are often taken by otherwise law-abiding individuals who may have the opportunity. People justify their actions in all kinds of ways, the most common one being that the recently deceased 'would have wanted me to have it anyway...' Even though you won't have authority to transfer money, empty bank accounts or make changes to any accounts (unless they are joint accounts or accounts that have what is called a 'transfer on death' notice attached to them) your job is to do all you can to protect those assets (the eggs) until they are ready to hatch.

TRANSFER ON DEATH ACCOUNTS

In estate planning, there is a little-used method to avoid probate called transfer on death (TOD) accounts. The moment the owner of a brokerage account or a piece of property dies, the account immediately becomes the property of the named individual. Up until that moment, the beneficiary has no rights, but immediately upon death they inherit the property without having to go through a probate process.

For people who like to plan in advance and, for whatever reason, don't want to put together a living trust, the transfer on death account gives them the opportunity to name a person who would receive property (real property, personal property or accounts) upon their death. It can be done with a vehicle through the DMV, and it can be done with real property by recording a deed at the county level. With bank accounts (often savings accounts or CD's), it's called payable on death (POD) designations.

Few people ever take such steps, so it is unlikely that you will confront a TOD or POD account, but it does happen, and it may be something you'll need to look into if you are a named executor or personal representative. How would you find out? You may need to do a little digging.

A preliminary title report ordered from a title company on real property will readily disclose a TOD designation, and getting such a report would always be a good idea. Through your local DMV, you can do a title search for a vehicle, and they'll send you a letter within a few weeks telling you who has legal title. Even though you are unlikely to find a TOD designation on a car or piece of real property, going through the steps to determine legal ownership is still worth doing.

TOD and POD accounts and deeds are fully revocable by the owner of the accounts at any time during their life, so even if someone went to the trouble of setting those designations up, there is no guarantee that they didn't change their mind at some point. The only way to know for sure is to do title searches and/or get current statements from the financial institutions in question.

DISTRIBUTING ASSETS & FENDING OFF CREDITORS
You will not be distributing assets from a probate estate until the court has issued letters of testamentary, and you have completed all of the business of the estate and submit to the court a final accounting and request to distribute

assets to heirs. Even though you won't be distributing assets until the very end of the probate process, you will have an obligation to keep paying bills that are due and to protect and preserve assets such as investment accounts and real property. Things may get thorny if and when you have people making claims on the estate for things which are not actually owed.

This may come as a surprise, but I see it happen on a very regular basis. Former friends and business associates of the deceased will literally come out of the woodwork to lay claim to assets or submit invoices for work never performed. It's almost comical what you see some people attempt to do! Who knew that Grandpa Joe had borrowed $10,000 from his good friend Bill, on a hand shake, with whom he played cards and that Bill now wants it all back - with interest...

This is an email message I received from a client during a trust litigation case where I was helping to administer the exit from a leased business space. The email message exemplifies how people attempt to make false claims to an estate. In this example, the landlord to my client's deceased father's shop was positioning himself to claim his property was contaminated by oil spilled maintaining service vehicles for the business: *"Just so you know it's my understanding that my Dad paid for and had poured the concrete slab that the rigs sit on in the back of the shop. He did this because if the rigs leaked oil or something that it would go on the slab he paid for. The concrete slab just improved his property if that is possible. If I were him I would be more concerned about the 100 plus wild cats and all the used cars, or the illegal caretaker that is hooked up to dads shop electricity. But in death, people like to get what they can get, or so I am learning the hard way. Holly said the landlord has never said a word ever to dad and trust me when dad ran his company it was 100 times more messy than it is now."*

With a little digging, I uncovered the fact the landlord's property was sitting on an EPA designated Superfund site, which the landlord failed to disclose to the tenant. What is creepy about this situation is the tenant was a personal friend of the landlord, yet he was attempting to make a false claim against the estate of his friend.

Do not assume that any bills submitted to the estate are bona fide. In this case, the burden of proof resides on the person submitting, and if there isn't documented evidence to support a claim, you should reject such shenanigans out of hand.

Yes, you do need to keep the utilities paid, and keeping the insurance current for cars and houses is critical. You do have an obligation as a personal representative, whether you have your letters of testamentary in hand or not, to make sure that you take reasonable steps to protect property. You may wait 30-45 days for a court hearing after submitting a petition to open probate, and the probate process can go slower than expected for all kinds of reasons, but in the interim utilities and insurance and mortgage payments are not the kinds of bills that you should ignore. You won't have authority to pay utilities, insurance, or mortgages but as a practical matter you better do it, or at minimum let the creditors know the debtor is deceased and they will likely work with you.

PROTECTING REAL PROPERTY WHEN SOMEONE IS STILL LIVING THERE

Very often people die, and a relative or close friend is living in their house with them. Particularly for people who aren't incapacitated but who need to be supervised, living in their own home (usually one that is paid for with no mortgage) with a caretaker or caregiver is a good compromise. But problems occur because in such cases there is hardly ever a rental agreement, and getting them out of the house if they're not willing to leave on their own, will require an 'unlawful detainer' also known as eviction proceedings. In California, a person who resides in a legally designated housing unit for ten or more consecutive days is legally afforded rights of tenancy. Note that getting an unlawful detainer when there is no written rental agreement will take even more time and expense than usual.

At a minimum, getting someone to leave a house who was living there to take care of a person who has since died, will take a minimum of 60 days' notice to quit the property. When they don't quit the property, you can hire an attorney and file an unlawful detainer action, but that will also take time. In the meantime, you will probably be sitting there watching the house get pilfered, personal property being taken out and sold, as well as people going in and trashing the house. Expect to have the property tied up in tenancy for 4 to 12 months, depending on how astute the squatter is on matters of tenancy law before you obtain an enforceable judgment for eviction. The process of removing unwanted tenants requires expertise, if you make mistakes in the eviction process you may have to start all over again from step one. I highly recommend that you employ professional real estate managers and attorneys who specialize in residential or commercial evictions to remove unwanted tenants.

Evicting unwanted tenants will be incredibly frustrating, and the practical reality is that there isn't anything you can do but execute the necessary steps until the court issues a judgment in your favor to receive possession of your property.

Although it seems unfair and unjust, in situations where someone is living in the house of a decedent and was there at the request of that person before they died, getting them out may pose problems. Unless and until you have legal standing to remove someone from a property, they have rights that will be protected.

If the property is in a trust, or if a property has a TOD status and will not go through probate, a trustee or beneficiary can request that anyone still living there vacate the house, but proper notice would still need to be given.

Locking down the assets of an estate while beneficiaries have ready access to those assets, is a certain recipe for abuse. Bad things can happen and usually do. If all of the above sounds bleak, unfortunately, there is little that can be done. That said, it may help to at least know what you are likely to encounter.

SMALL BUSINESSES IN PROBATE

If someone is self-employed or owns a small business, and you are probating or managing their estate, you first need to take a hard look at the business and decide how viable it is, and if there is anything there with lasting value. I estimate that a majority of the time, for people who are self-employed, their business will simply fold. There may be requirements to formally close out an LLC or S-Corp, which is something you should talk over with an attorney and a qualified tax consultant, but there isn't often a business worth preserving when the "key" person has died.

Sometimes, however, there are businesses that are ongoing with demand and may even have employees. Did anyone work in the business who might want to take it over? That's the first question I would ask. The estate may work out a deal to sell the business to that person on favorable terms - not necessarily a favorable price, as the price needs to be the market price, but financing terms can certainly be arranged to make it easier for an employee to become an owner. If there's a way to get cash out for the beneficiaries, that's worth pursuing. Protecting the business assets in a timely fashion is paramount when there are employees. Changing locks to warehouses and offices to protect business assets and to control access to property and records of value is critical. Once thieves start pillaging property, records, accounts receivables and cash the chances of recovery are *slim*. This is evidenced by an email communication I received from a frustrated client trying to protect her deceased father's business: "Well Dan, as far as I know, all customers are ok. I haven't heard from anyone. I will remain squeaky clean, but please explain how someone like Felicity can Keep and sell ALL of my dad's stuff other than the business and a few old broken-down vehicles...with NO consequences whatsoever. It never ceases to amaze me that criminals get away with stuff I would be put in jail for."

Transferring a business after the owner has died can sometimes be complicated, especially if there are special licenses involved. I was recently involved in a receivership case where the business owner was required to hold a special license issued by the state. It was a viable business, but the family didn't have any members who had the license and could, therefore, run the operation. There was, however, a key employee who was interested in buying it, and the attorney who was representing the trust told me about the situation. My recommendation was to go to court and seek the appointment of a receiver who could operate the business until the key employee could get the necessary license to take over. Inserting a court-appointed receiver is a great way to preserve the value and ongoing day to day operations of a business until a qualified buyer can be found.

Taking care of a small business is just the same as managing real estate or managing a portfolio of investments. The obligation is to protect and preserve, and you need to be proactive in that. With businesses, however, it can be a little more difficult to know what needs to be paid, what needs to be challenged or re-negotiated, and what decisions will be best for the long-term survival of the entity. If the business won't survive on autopilot, you may have limited amounts of time to figure things out. There's no sin in asking for help, and I encourage anyone in this situation to reach out to anyone they know with great business acumen to get advice and counsel. If the situation calls for it, hire a temporary manager or business consultant, but above all try not to let the ship sink!

CHAPTER SUMMARY:

- Don't wait for letters and court approvals. Do whatever you can to protect the assets of an estate.
- Protecting real property may mean changing the locks and keeping valuables locked up.
- Some small businesses may be viable after the owner dies, but most will not be. Seek out professional advice and assistance if the issue is in doubt.

9

Performance Bonds

In some cases, a Probate Court may require someone to obtain a performance bond. Performance bonds, which are also known as surety bonds, are essentially pledges that the person undertaking an act on behalf of another will faithfully perform their duties. If they do things that are negligent or illegal or violate their fiduciary obligations in a way that harms others, a bond gives some recourse to those who were harmed. There is some risk for the underwriter of that bond. If the bonded person does something wrong, the bonding agent stands ready to pay the full face value of the bond as settlement towards damages that have been inflicted or sustained.

When you are being considered as an administrator, and even potentially as an executor, the person whose estate is being administered may have specifically stated that the executor of their estate not be required to post a bond. Even though the decedent may have made such a request, the Probate Court may not consider you to be trustworthy, completely responsible, or you simply lack experience. Ultimately, the court still has the discretion to require that a bond be posted despite a will or trust stating no bonding will be required of the executor or trustee.

Why would a Probate Court require a bond? Here are two common reasons:

- The court thinks the person named as executor is not fully qualified in areas where the court feels oversight and protection would be prudent.
- A 3rd party is being appointed, and the court believes that the beneficiaries and heirs need to be protected. If you are an unrelated person to the estate, you will very likely be required to post a performance bond.

If a Probate Court decides that you need to be bonded, the judge will set an amount that he or she believes is warranted - that amount is totally at the discretion of the judge. In most receivership cases I take on, for example, I look at the value of the assets I will be managing and make a recommendation to the judge for what my bond should be. In most such cases, I have found that judges typically agree with my recommendation, but they don't have to. Before I am permitted to take any action, however, I am always required to post a bond, which may be $10,000 on the low end or $100,000+ on the high end.

Obtaining a performance bond is usually not difficult. There are quite a few bonding companies to choose from, and it's easy enough to find them online. You would fill out what is akin to a loan application, and the bonding company does a background check and a credit check. If you meet their underwriting criteria, the bonding company will offer to issue a bond, and the charge they will assess will depend on a few criteria: your history of being bonded, your credit score and any criminal history and experience in the duties you will be performing. As with most forms of insurance, the greater risk you are, the more it will cost you to obtain a bond. A typical charge is $5/thousand, up to $250,000 in coverage; a $100,000 bond would cost ~$500.

A performance bond once pledged, is essentially a guarantee from a bonding company that if something goes wrong, they will pay the claim. You should think of it as an insurance policy with a certain level of monetary value is being held in reserve if the person who is bonded does something negligent or is unable to complete the work, which is why they call it a performance bond.

The cost of getting a bond is typically the cost of doing the estate business and is often not chargeable to the probate estate. Do not assume that the estate will reimburse you for the expense. That said, once everything is wrapped up and a final accounting is presented to the court, you will generally be permitted to request reimbursement. Whether the court decides to allow reimbursement or not is entirely up to the judge. Of course, the bonding company itself will never give you your money back.

HOW TO FIND A BONDING COMPANY
The easiest way to find a bonding company is to type in 'bonding company, probate' on the web browser of your phone or computer, and a long list of companies will come up. Note that you don't necessarily need to find one in your own city or even state. You can be bonded by a company anywhere in the country, and they can issue a

performance or surety bond regardless of your geographic location.

Some clerk of courts may provide a list of bonding companies that they regularly do business with, and it's fair to assume that any company on the list is reputable. You don't need to work from that list, but it's often a good place to start.

Should you get multiple bids to find the lowest cost performance bond? In my opinion, two bids would be enough. Remember that each time you apply for a bond, the company will probably pull a credit report. The more inquiries, the more your score will go down. If you're concerned about your credit score, you might try to find companies that pull a so-called soft report, which would not have an impact on your credit.

The criteria used by bonding companies are extremely similar, so it is unlikely that you will save more than $100, or maybe $200, by shopping around. If you have the time, there isn't any reason why you couldn't get five or even ten quotes, but in most cases, you wouldn't want to do that! To get a firm and accurate quote, you're going to need to fill out an application and submit it for underwriting. Even if there are stated rates you can easily find, those rates will not be guaranteed. The rate you will be charged will depend on your assets, debts, credit, criminal history, and background.

There are ways to self-bond or self-insure without using a bonding company, but to meet the level of assurance required for an assurance bond, it would not be easy to set up. At the end of the day, it would take far more work, and end up being more expensive, to self-insure so I would not recommend trying to do that.

CHAPTER SUMMARY:
- If you are not directly related to the decedent, you should expect that you will be required to post a bond.
- Getting bonded isn't difficult, but you should shop around.
- Self-bonding (or self-insuring) is probably never a good idea.

10

How to Inventory Estate Assets

I n earlier chapters, I've mentioned all the benefits to getting a fee appraisal for real property and attaching that as an exhibit to the initial petition to open probate. Let me reiterate that that is an important, and oft-over-looked, first step.

There may be instances where the Clerk of the Court will reject the fee appraisal with the initial petition. More than likely, rejection would be due to a clerical issue, such as if the fee appraisal is addressed to someone who does not yet have standing in the court. At the initial filing, of course, there won't yet be a personal representative. Once you receive your letters of testamentary, you will have standing in the eyes of the court to conduct business, but before receiving those letters, you don't technically have standing.

Sometimes clerks may be sticklers on the point and may tell you that a fee appraisal addressed to someone who does not have standing can't be submitted. Other times clerks will accept a document at the counter, but you'll get a phone call from a clerk stating the Probate Examiner won't accept the document and they want you to come back and pick it up. Even with the chance that could happen, I still advise anyone to get a fee appraisal immediately and to submit that appraisal with the initial documents to open probate. You can refile the appraisal report as an amendment to your petition for probate after you have been appointed and received your letters of testamentary. Have your attorney help you with a cover sheet noting the case number and other pertinent headings to properly identify the document as part of your probate case.

If you know a real estate agent that you may want to work with, or a loan broker, or a banker, call and ask them for a referral to a licensed appraiser who knows the area. You can also find appraisers with an Internet search. You'll need to ask them first, if they have time to issue an appraisal in the short amount of time you'll have (usually less than 30 days, but residential appraisers typically have quick turnaround times), and second, how much an appraisal will cost. In California, a fee appraisal generally costs between $400 and $600. You should also ask your appraiser to render an opinion about market trends for the subject property. If you're not looking to sell the property right away, and you get an opinion that the market is trending up, you may need to consider the tax implications of holding on to the property. So, for example, if you get a fee appraisal at the time of death which says that a property is worth $400,000, but you don't sell it until a year later when it might be worth $450,000, the net difference (less selling costs) may be considered taxable income to the beneficiaries of the property sale. If having to pay taxes on a gain is a consideration, this is something to keep in mind. On the flip side, if the market is going down, and the property is likely to sell for less than the appraised value at the time of death, then tax consequences will tend to be less of a concern.

Do you ever need two appraisals? Probably not. But if you are ever interested in getting a second opinion, my advice would be to invite a real estate agent to come and inspect the property in order to give you a comparative market analysis or a broker price opinion. Incidentally, a broker price opinion is an alternative to a fee appraisal, and you can get a letter from a real estate broker that will serve as a defensible valuation with a Probate Court. The reason I recommend a fee appraisal over a market analysis is because fee appraisals use principles of real property valuation in the appraisal, whereas a comparative market analysis relies primarily upon comparable sales. If you want to save $400+ dollars, you can ask a real estate broker to come and inspect the property and give you a market analysis, which you can use an alternative to submit as an exhibit with your initial petition to open probate.

Whether you get a fee appraisal or a comparative market analysis, I would recommend that you have it addressed to whoever is named in the will to be the executor. If there is no will and your case is an intestate filing I would have it addressed to the prospective administrator. Yes, there is a chance that person will not be named, but it is still worth including the appraisal with your initial petition to open probate. By filing early, with the initial petition, you stand a good chance of influencing the probate referee to go along with whatever number your appraiser comes up with. Either way, you are using higher standards to establish an actual market value of a property than what a probate referee would be able to come up with in a cursory 'drive-by' appraisal and Zillow, which is notoriously inaccurate in the opinion of real estate brokers who are in the trenches every day. You will be much better off if you can influence the probate referee's number to more accurately reflect market conditions.

DO YOU ALWAYS WANT THE HIGH APPRAISAL?

The short answer is yes because you want the heirs of the state to benefit from a stepped-up basis of value! The Probate Court is always going to want to see that the subject property sells for at least 90% of whatever number the probate referee comes up with. If your appraisal says $200,000, the probate referee says $150,000, and the property sells for $175,000, is that a problem? Probably not, because the selling price is still more than 90% of the probate referee's appraisal. Don't you have a taxable gain on the difference? In fact, you probably would not. In this case, if anything, you could argue that you have a taxable loss because you established the fair market value of the property at $200,000 on the date of death, but you were only able to sell it for $175,000. If you had relied solely on the probate referee to provide a tax basis, then you might be on the hook for a tax gain due to poor valuation by a probate referee, who charges you as much money as fee appraisal but with inferior work product. In the reverse situation, where the market is devaluing, a higher appraiser will potentially result in a 'net loss' for taxation purposes upon distribution on your personal tax return. Those 'losses' are only paper losses because you are receiving a gift, but they result in real dollar tax savings later.

Look at it this way: If you have a property that the probate referee values at $400,000, your fee appraisal comes in at $500,000, but the property ultimately sells for $600,000, instead of having a $200,000 potential gain to report to the

IRS, you will have only $100,000, because you can support the argument that the house was worth $500,000 and not $400,000. Even in a worst-case scenario where the probate examiner rejects your appraisal, having that fee appraisal, from a tax perspective, in establishing a new basis of value in a property, you have complied with best practices in valuation for the estate. The IRS, when looking at a probate referee appraisal versus a fee appraisal, will almost always accept the fee appraisal as the most accurate value because all the elements of valuation are employed in a fee appraisal.

WHAT AND WHEN TO LIQUIDATE

You will not be allowed to liquidate anything in a probate estate until you have received letters of testamentary. Once you have received those, and if you are given full authority, you will have the ability (and the obligation) to conduct the business of the estate. In most cases, your primary consideration will be the preservation of value, which means that you will want to liquidate anything which may be worth less the longer you hold it.

What about Grandpa's 2000 shares of AT&T? Any stock, no matter how apparently solid, is affected by market forces. Unless your name is Warren Buffett, the chances are good that you will not be able to tell whether those shares are likely to be worth more in a year than they are today. True, you could be foregoing a significant gain if you sell and the market goes up. The risk/reward calculus in probate matters, however, always favors the risk side: you should always sell any stocks, and probably most bonds (unless they are Treasury securities) that are in the estate as soon as you are allowed to do so.

Consider that if you think you can time the market, and you guess wrong, you may be held liable by the other beneficiaries of the estate for losing their money when you had a chance not to do so. Beneficiaries can't sue you if you sell too soon to realize date of death value, but they can surely sue you if you sell too late and below, date of death value. In either case, you won't be able to distribute the proceeds from any sales, but you will be preserving wealth, which is your primary fiduciary duty.

The inventory of what's in the estate is something that you'll want to tackle early for several reasons. First, if you have a lot of family in the area, and you have family members with financial issues or substance abuse issues, and they are coming in and out of the home, you risk the very real possibility that those people will walk out the door with estate assets. It may be helpful to prove that the assets existed (through an inventory) than trying to argue that you think you saw something but can't prove it.

What happens if your cousin Joe does go into the house and walks out with a silver bowl belonging to your late mother? How can you get it back? Unfortunately, things like this happen all the time - in fact, I venture to say that in more than 90% of all estates, someone takes something of value either right before or right after a death has occurred. It's incredibly common.

Once someone walks away with something from the decedent, personal objects of any kind, be they jewelry, art, collectibles, or currency, it is incredibly difficult, and for practical purposes impossible, to ever get them back. An inventory might prove that an object is missing, and you might even have video proof of someone stealing an object, but there are few realistically affordable, or practical processes or procedures for getting it back. You can call the police, but in most cases, your local police will not have time or interest to investigate the theft of an object from an estate, they will likely tell you it is a civil matter.

If such an event has already happened, my best advice is just to let it go. As difficult as it will be for someone to hear that advice, the emotional turmoil, energy and expense that will be expended, and the extremely low probability of an object ever being recovered, really need to be considered. Even in my own family, when my mother died, I discovered that some members had taken objects that didn't belong to them. In the end, I got no satisfaction, no return of stolen property, and no closure. I can say honestly and from personal experience that you need to move past such events for your own mental health. Seriously, don't focus on that stuff - it can make people truly unhinged.

Which isn't to say that you shouldn't do everything possible to prevent people from taking property from the deceased. If someone is about to die, and you are there at the time, you need to do everything possible to lock down their property, and by 'lock down' I do mean physically lock things down. Hire a locksmith and get the locks changed. If there are extremely valuable objects, you might consider hiring a private security detail to watch the property and keep everyone out. You have to secure the property of the estate, and limiting access is one of the most effective ways of doing so. This is another good reason to install video cameras to cover exit doors from the property. The best way to make sure that the assets of an estate are distributed to the appropriate beneficiaries is to do everything possible to protect those assets at the moment they become your responsibility. Failure to act, or failure to act quickly will likely cause irreparable damage for which you may find yourself personally liable. Better to be safe, not sorry.

CHAPTER SUMMARY:

- Always get your own appraisal for any real property that will be going through probate, I cannot stress this point enough.
- A high appraisal estimate is never going to be a problem in taxation, in fact it may help reduce beneficiary tax if they show a 'paper loss' on the liquidation.
- Your fiduciary responsibility means that you should do whatever you can to protect the assets of an estate. Do not, for example, try to time the stock market. Sell liquid assets the first opportunity you are allowed to do so; it is your best protection in one of the most risk-related duties you have as a Personal Representative or Trustee to an estate.

11

Creditors

fter you have filed your petition to open a probate, you're going to have a hearing, usually within 30 to 45 days. At that hearing, you're going to be issued your letters of testamentary, and shortly afterward, you will be required to notice known or, potential, creditors. Usually, you will want to take care of that requirement within 30 days or sooner, if possible. There are statutory requirements for how creditors must be noticed, and your attorney can help you with that.

When the court gives you a Hearing date for your petition to probate, you will need to provide notice of the hearing to certain persons who have an interest in the estate, e.g., heirs and beneficiaries, so they know the time and date of the hearing. The other written notice a PR must provide is to known, or to potential, creditors. A personal representative is not liable to a creditor for failure to give written notice unless it is done in bad faith. In other words, you knew but failed to act. However, the burden of proving bad faith is upon the person or the entity seeking to impose liability upon you. Keep that in mind; you may not want to learn more than you need to about the decedent's debts!

In working on probate cases for many years, there are a few places where courts tend to be very particular. First, the notice to creditors must be both mailed and published. Typically, it is cheapest to publish in periodicals that specialize in legal notices. You will need to pay special attention to make sure that you have complied with the statutory requirements for noticing creditors. If you fail to follow the procedures to the absolute letter, there is a good chance that the court will make you do the steps over. It may seem punitive and draconian, but the reality is that the systems put in place are there for a reason, and courts don't have the time or interest to accept variations from the standard. If it says that something must be published in a certain way and at a certain time, and done by a certain procedure, don't mess with it! Do it exactly as prescribed, or you will likely lose both time and money. I strongly recommend you employ competent legal counsel to help with your court required notices in probate, if you fail to provide all the necessary notices, in the required format and steps, you will have to repeat the process.

CREDIT CARDS AND OTHER UNSECURED DEBTS
Some self-help books on probate recommend that if the decedent had credit card debt, you should cut up their cards and mail them to the credit card companies with a certified copy of the death certificate. Without meaning to be too judgmental, I think that is a silly idea, and I would never recommend you do such a thing. You are a fiduciary when

you act as a personal representative or, as a trustee. Your duty is to protect and preserve the estate's assets, not the bank or credit card company's assets. Do not do more than the minimum required by statute to notify credit card companies.

My recommendation is you take some time, if the deceased had credit card debt, to work to reduce the balances owed to the credit card company. Sometimes, it is a simple as asking. Sometimes the credit card companies will forgive the debt, but otherwise, the estate may be required to pay it. In my experience, when I have requested credit card companies to reduce the balance because the debtor is deceased, they will often reduce the amount owed by 25% or sometimes more, if the deceased did not have much money when they died. So, be sure to ask the question if the balance can be adjusted to a lower amount given the fact the person has died.

In noticing creditors, my recommendation is to request your attorney's firm mail required notices to creditors, in California, the court requires the notice be prepared and mailed by a third party, you are not allowed to "self-notice." The PR or trustee can handle the required step to publish notices to creditors in a local public periodical, as duly required. In noticing creditors, absolutely do not do more than you are legally required to. Do not mail credit card companies death certificates, and don't cut up the cards and mail them back. All of that is just wasted effort.

You may not realize it, but credit bureaus (Experian, Equifax, and TransUnion) collect an enormous amount of information about you, whether you like it or not. They regularly and routinely sift through and collect all court documents through a third-party company called Lexis-

Nexis. As soon as a probate case has been opened, those credit reporting agencies will have access to Probate Court filings via Lexis-Nexis. That legal service information is available to all three credit bureaus, and they may note on the credit file that the owner is reported deceased before you even provide notice to them.

In the case of joint accounts, yes, you should contact the credit card company directly to report that a joint account holder has died. The remaining person(s) on the account will still be liable for whatever outstanding balance exists. They may ask you to send a certified copy of the death certificate. Even just calling them is essentially a courtesy because they would find out sooner or later from the credit bureaus.

So, what happens if someone dies owing $20,000 in credit card debt, and you don't contact the credit card company? After 120 days of non-payment, the credit card company will write off the account and send it to collections. At that point, the deceased person's credit score will drop quite dramatically. As it turns out, creditors typically have 120 days to file a claim against an estate after they have received notice from the PR or the trustee. After that date, if no claim has been filed, they'll be out of luck -- the estate will not be obligated to pay the creditor.

Your obligation is to comply with the statutes and post the required notices. That's it. So why would anyone notify a credit card company beyond the minimum statutory requirement? If you call the company directly, of course, they will tell you that the estate must pay any outstanding balance, but the reality is that it's unlikely that a Probate Court will care.

On undocumented debts owed to the deceased, once someone dies, that debt is, for practical purposes, uncollectible in most cases. If there is no legal requirement to call the decedent's undocumented debtors, I suggest that you don't bother; you will only serve to frustrate yourself.

Unsecured debts are lowest on the priority list for any probate estate, which means that there would be a lot of paperwork and possible legal expense to collect what might ultimately be pennies on the dollar.

Here's the bottom line: You should always let unsecured creditors be responsible for their own obligations after you have given proper notice. You don't need to go out of your way to help them. That said, if you're talking about unsecured debts from the gardener or the pool cleaner, those are moral judgments, and I would say that those people should be paid ahead of any bank or credit card company.

Utilities can sometimes also fall into the category of unsecured debt, but the difference here is that you may need to keep paying them if you want to use them. Utility companies are often quasi-government agencies, since most have monopoly status, and I have seen them be tenacious bill collectors. If you still need gas, electric or water/sewer services, you may need to make peace with them, and you should expect to pay them accordingly.

For claims such as gym memberships, or club memberships, where a 30-day notice to quit is usually required, I would tend to ignore those. If you send such companies a certified copy of a death certificate with a letter stating that the member has died, few legitimate operators will press their claim.

WHAT ABOUT CLAIMS THAT ARE NOT VALID?

Usually, the types of people who file claims that are not valid are 'mom and pop operators' who see an opportunity and try to take advantage of a situation. In smaller communities, when someone passes away who is by all accounts wealthy, it is both comical and typical that their estates will receive claims for all kinds of goods and services that were never delivered or provided. Interestingly enough, when they find out that they will have to go before a judge to assert their claims, a lot of such people opt to let things drop.

Recently I sent out a notice to potential creditors in a Trust estate, and I got several phone calls from former employees who had worked for the company owned by the decedent. They made claims that they had left tools at the man's shop that they had never gotten back, and they described the tools in great detail. When I asked them to provide some evidence that the tools were theirs, anything such as a receipt, a credit card statement, or anything else that would show that they bought them and had a claim to them, they could never produce any paperwork. I also invited them to show up at a hearing before the court. Again, in all the years I've been doing this, no one with such claims has ever come forward.

If you find people coming out of the woodwork to ask for compensation, my advice is to ask them to bring any evidence or documentation they may have to the next scheduled Probate Court hearing. In this way, you don't necessarily have to be 'the bad guy' by telling someone that their claim is bogus, and you don't believe them. Let the Probate Court process work for you. If they can indeed prove their claim, the court and the judge will gladly compensate them. If not, that's one less problem for you.

For someone to make a valid claim, there has to be some level of provenance that someone can produce. Even the most honest-looking and earnest person appearing before a judge with no evidence except a good story will likely have their claim rejected. That's just how the system works. If there is no supporting evidence, as ruled by the Probate Court, the estate will not be obligated to pay. If there is evidence, however, and if it is within the statutory period for a claim to be put forward, then the estate should probably pay the claim. When such situations come up, it is always advisable to consult with an attorney to make certain that both the rule and letter of the law are being followed.

CHAPTER SUMMARY:

- Do not do anything more than you are legally required to do in noticing potential creditors.
- If a credit card company or an unsecured creditor files a claim after the statutory cut-off date, and if you have followed the law for noticing all claimants, you can safely ignore them.
- The onus to prove a claim is on the claimant.
- Anyone who makes what you believe to be an invalid claim should be asked to provide written evidence and be prepared to present that evidence to the court.

12

Taxes

F ew tasks in life are as thankless and frustrating as doing your taxes. Software programs can streamline the process, but tax laws are complex and complicated, and the nuances can be important. Filing a tax return for an estate is even more difficult, mostly because you may not know some basic information that could be relevant, such as cost basis or deductible expenses.

Let me save you a lot of time and money. Yes, in most cases, you should hire a CPA.

If you are administering an estate that has real property assets, securities or other assets whose value may be discretionary, you will absolutely want to hire a CPA. A Certified Public Accountant, especially one who has experienced in the filing of fiduciary returns, will not only make sure that the returns are accurate, but will also make sure that you file the correct and proper returns within the required amount of time. In my experience, there are CPAs who specialize in fiduciary returns, and those who do not. If you already work with a CPA who has little experience in this area, he or she may refer you to another tax professional.

Within 24 hours of when someone dies, it is important that someone notify the Social Security Administration that they have died. Often, the funeral home will make the report – you just need to make sure you give them the Social Security number. Note that the Social Security Administration will want to receive a copy of the death certificate, but the funeral home will probably take care of that if you request it.

At the same time, you need to request a new Tax ID number from the IRS for the estate. Online, you can obtain a new tax identification number for the estate of the deceased immediately. Why is it so important to get a new Tax ID? Without a Tax ID number, you will not be able to open a bank account for the estate or transact any of the other necessary business.

When it comes to filing taxes for the estate of someone who has died, there are three types of tax returns:

1.) The deceased, if they had income in the calendar year of their death must file a 1040 Form Individual Tax Return to report income and expenses up to the date of death.
2.) If the deceased makes income post date of death, that income is to be reported on a 1041 Form Income Tax Return for Estates and Trusts. As an example, even if brokerage accounts issue 1099 or 1098 income to the individual for earned income after the date of death that income is still reported on the 1041 Form Income Tax Return for Estates and Trusts, not the 1040 Form Individual Tax Return.
3.) If the gross value of the estate exceeds $11,200,000 you must file 706 United States Estate (and Generation-Skipping Transfer) Tax Return, also known as the "estate tax return." Estate tax returns are only required if the gross value of the estate meets or

exceeds $11,200,000, and it indexes annually from 2018 to adjust for inflation.

One critical issue that many people get wrong. The timing of when to file is often important. If someone dies in March, for example, you will need to file a tax return for that person for the duration of the calendar year for which they were alive, e.g., by the end of February of the following year. You will also need to file a fiduciary or estate return for that same year. The estate is created on the date of death, that date becomes the estate's tax calendar year date unless you opt for a fiscal year versus a calendar year, but either way, it cannot be longer than a year.

A 706 Form Return should be filed within 9-months if the estate's gross value exceeds the eleven million dollars benchmark. You may file an extension for the 706 Form Return for up to 15 months.

Note that an estate's tax return tax filing date is not cast in stone, there are (limited) options, especially if there are complications. If, for example, the estate holds assets that cannot be liquidated within the tax year, you may want to get an extension. A CPA would be able to advise you on the pros and cons of filing at specific times, and you want to get it right.

SHOULD YOU ALSO HIRE A BOOKKEEPER?

If you can keep track and organize the estate debts and obligations, then you may not need a bookkeeper. Even if you are good with keeping track of expenses, you can probably find a bookkeeper who is QuickBooks certified for $20 to $45 per hour. In my opinion, that would be money well spent, because an experienced bookkeeper will put all your expenses and debts into categories that can easily be used by your CPA to create a tax return.

In fact, you may ultimately save money by hiring a bookkeeper because they will take some of the burden off your CPA, whose hourly rate is likely to be $100 to $200 per hour. Either way, you should anticipate spending at least $1,000 to file a fiduciary tax return and as much as $4,000, or more, if the return is complicated. You don't need to be a math genius to figure this one out!

It is important that you (or your bookkeeper, or your CPA) keep meticulous records to track those expenses. Failure to keep accurate records may cause delays and additional expenses. You may believe that the Probate Court will never comb through expenses to determine which are legitimate and which are not. If so, you would be wrong. In my experience, Probate Courts are adept at spotting erroneous or padded expenses. The penalties can be stiff, so I advise keeping accurate records.

TAX ISSUES THAT MAY REQUIRE COURT APPROVAL
In most cases, Probate Court approval is not needed for any tax issues, but what you do need to be aware of is that the estate administration expenses that are essential to the administration and settlement of the estate, must be approved by the court to discharge a probate estate. Your final accounting, which you will need to file when you petition to have the probate case closed, will have to itemize all those expenses. Approval by the court is not the same as approval by the Internal Revenue Service; ultimately, the IRS must be satisfied the return(s) are accurate to close out an estate.

An example of a tax issue that could need court approval is medical expenses. It turns out that medical expenses are the one item that can be deducted before they are actually paid. That raises the question: where do you want to apply those medical expenses? Do you want to apply them to the last return for the individual, or do you want to apply them to the Form 706 for large value estates? That's where you should really get professional tax advice to determine if medical expenses should accrue to the individual or, if the expense is large enough, the large estate 706 Form return.

Tax choices may seem arbitrary, but the implications can be huge depending on which option is taken. An individual tax rate may be as low as 0%, whereas any estate taxes that are due will be taxed at 40%. In most cases this won't be an issue, because the threshold for taxes in 2018 is an estate with assets in excess of $11.2 million, and the Trump tax code changes raise federal taxation to estates with gross value of $11.2 million or more, but you will always want to do whatever you legally can to minimize the amount of taxes owed. Get with your tax consultant early and before you liquidate high-value assets is my recommendation for best fiduciary practices.

To give you a sense of how complexities arise, and issues can combine in estates, consider an estate with both medical expenses and a real estate holding - a situation that is extremely common. Suppose someone owned a condo worth $200,000 on the date of death. By the time you are able to sell the condo, it may then be worth $250,000. In that case, the estate would have a gain of $50,000. Once the estate is distributed, following a Probate Court approval, that taxable event would be distributed on a percentage basis to those heirs who received the proceeds. However, if you can apply medical expenses to the estate tax return, and assuming that's a significant number, it could be used to offset some or all of the gains that would otherwise fall to the beneficiaries.

Note that if an estate has income that exceeds $600 in a calendar year, there is a legal requirement to file a tax return. So, there may be returns that are filed on behalf of the estate prior to the final return. In the case of my mother's estate, which was a trust estate, it took three years to ultimately settle her estate. In the interim, I filed three tax returns, plus her private return in the calendar year of her death, so in total, over a three-year period, I filed four returns for her estate. As a rule of thumb, selling large value estate assets triggers filing requirements, and an experienced Fiduciary Tax Return Preparer is the best counsel you can seek.

The most important tax break implication about inheritance is, Stepped Up Basis. What does stepped up basis mean? It means the date of death value of large assets is the new tax valuation basis you inherit as a beneficiary. This can work for you or, it can work against you, depending on the economic conditions at the time of death. An example would be if your parent had bought an income property in 2005 that was worth $2.2 million, and they died in 2009, that same income property may have only been worth $1.3 million. That means if you later sold that same property at a later date for $2.2 million you would, in simplistic terms, have a gain of $900 thousand, even though your parent paid $2.2 million for that same property. In periods where asset values are increasing, if your parent bought the same property for $2.2 million, and at the date of death that same property is worth $3.6 million, you could sell that asset for $4.0 million, and your gain would only be $400,000 versus $1.4 million.

Strategies in distribution also come into play with taxation. An example, individual retirement accounts (IRA's), because they are tax-deferred investment vehicles. With IRA's it is best to name direct beneficiaries because you have greater flexibility to defer tax consequences to match individual needs, e.g., a high income earning sibling may not want to incur another $100,000 in income where another lower earning sibling would want to liquidate and pay tax at a lower individual rate than their high earning sibling.

By this point, I hope you now see that tax issues can be complicated, which means that it's easy to make mistakes. Why take the chance? If you can hire a well-qualified tax professional, I strongly suggest that you do so. We can't avoid death or taxes, but we should do whatever we can to delay the first and minimize the latter!

CHAPTER SUMMARY:

- You will ultimately save yourself time and money by hiring a good CPA (one who knows how to file estate tax returns) and a good bookkeeper (one who has worked on estates).
- Get good and competent accounting advice before selling high value assets or filing tax returns for either the decedent or the estate.
- What may seem like inconsequential issues may be worth tens of thousands of dollars in tax dollars saved or spent.

13

When Trustees or Personal Representatives Loan Money to an Estate

I recently consulted on a litigation matter where opposing counsel tendered an offer to settle the dispute. When the attorney presented the terms of settlement to our client, he objected that his sibling, who was the trustee of the trust he had a beneficial interest in, was being reimbursed for a significant amount of personal funds she loaned while administering the trust through some rocky slopes. Part of her personal funds was used to protect the trust from a possible foreclosure for an income property owned by the trust. This trustee was fortunate to be able to prevent the property from being foreclosed, but should she have used her own money to do so?

I would never advise a trustee or administrator to use their personal funds if they can avoid it. The reason is that it is not an administrator's duty to personally pay for estate obligations, especially when there are multiple beneficiaries. If you are acting as the estate administrator and you are also the sole beneficiary, then it may well be appropriate to use your own funds but bear in mind that you need to keep good records.

I have a phrase which I often share in matters of administering estates, whether it is a probate or trust; and the phrase is, "no good deed goes unpunished." If you are acting as the fiduciary of a deceased family member's estate or trust, or even as a professionally licensed fiduciary, beneficiaries often do not understand, nor do they appreciate, when you use your personal financial resources, and assume personal risk, to fund an estate that has assets, but little or no cash.

In my work as a real estate broker assisting in the administration of an estate and sale of real property, I sometimes use my personal funds to cover critical expenses if the estate has no money. Even with all my experience, it doesn't always turn out well. I have found myself, on occasion, being out a large sum of money for long periods of time before I can be re-paid because of complexities in positioning properties to be "financeable" to fund an estate.

If you are a beneficiary to a probate or trust, and you are in conflict with the personal representative or the trustee, and they have loaned their own money when the estate lacked sufficient cash to settle the estate, understand that the personal representative or trustee is entitled to have their personal loan repaid, with reasonable interest, when it comes time to settle and distribute assets, if not sooner. I have seen beneficiaries assume the money loaned by the administrator or trustee becomes an estate asset versus an estate liability that needs to be repaid. Try not to allow your passionate conflict to color your good judgment, a loan to the estate, even from people you may conflict with, will still need to be repaid.

PRIVATE MONEY LOANS

One of the most common requests I receive in my real estate services business in matters of probate and trusts are requests from administrators and trustees to "fund the estate." What does that mean? Settling an estate requires money. If the decedent died without much or any cash, and I see this frequently, the administrator must find the necessary cash to pay the decedents' bills for everyday items like insurance and utilities, attorney's, real property taxes, funeral expenses, etc.

Real property can be an excellent asset to use as security for short-term loans to fund an estate sufficiently to administer an estate until final distributions can be made. Private money loans are a commonly used source of financing to fund estates.

Private money loans are typically brokered through licensed real estate brokers who have relationships with investors who offer to loan money at high-interest rates; today they range from 9.5% to 12% interest and loan points average 2-3%. Investors offer these loans because institutional banks, such as Bank of America or Chase, will not likely provide loans to fund estates.

There are two common categories of private money loans; business purpose loans and consumer loans. There are a lot of details to consider when financing an estate, and the best option is to seek a business loan versus a consumer loan. Note that you may seek a business purpose loan provided the money is being used solely to conduct the business of the estate.

The benefit of a business purpose loan is the trustee, or personal representative does not have to be personally liable to repay the loan, this is commonly referred as a "non-recourse loan." Besides dodging personal liability, non-recourse business loans are beneficial because the underwriting is far simpler and much quicker than a consumer loan. This is because the loan is made based upon the investor using the real property to secure their money loan, and credit scores of individuals do not factor in the decision.

To obtain more detailed information about private money loans, you may go to my website, http://www.collinsfiduciarybroker.
com/, and select the "Private Money Loans" tab. I am available to assist with helping you find sources of money to fund the estate you are administering through my affiliate relationships with private money lenders.

When you accept a private money loan secured by real property, you will most often use a title company to transact the funding of the loan. The investor will usually want the administrator or trustee to provide them with "title insurance" which insures the title to the property is in good standing, and that the personal representative or trustee has legal authority to encumber the real property. If you are probating the estate, the lender will want to see your Letters of Testamentary, or if you are a trustee, a Certification of Trust and perhaps a Certification of Trustee as well as a copy of the trust documents. Be prepared to provide certified copies of death certificates, for all persons who have died that were the on title of the real property.

Again, when the first spouse dies, unless they had a Living Trust, their estate must petition for probate before you will be able to sell or finance real property. Often, I am asked to provide multiple death certificates if title to the property shows more than one person's name. If the property is a held as joint tenancy with rights of survivorship, and there is a surviving spouse, family member or another party, that property will not be considered part of the estate and therefore cannot be financed using a business purpose loan. When in doubt, always consult your attorney.

CHAPTER SUMMARY

- Lending money to an estate can be a risky business, and you should never use your personal funds if you can avoid it.
- Private money loans are good options for estates or trusts holding real assets, but which are short on cash. As always, it pays to shop around.
- If you do decide to get a private money loan, always sign up for a business purpose, as the loan itself will be non-recourse and no credit checks will be required.

14

Disbursement of Assets in Probate

How do you know if you're ready or not? Timing to make distributions is one of the single largest differences between administering a trust, versus probate estate. Trust estates allow the trustee to make partial distributions at any time, with the flexibility to make unequal distributions if necessary, to accommodate beneficiaries' needs as they arise and within the trustee's comfort and ability to track accounts.

Conversely, in a probate, Executors must accomplish a series of steps before they are ready to file a final petition for distribution with the Probate Court. Before you can file that petition you must make sure that all the following steps were faithfully executed:

- Create (and submit) a complete accounting of assets, debts, taxes and remaining assets (net assets) remaining to heirs.

- Publish a public notice in a periodical that is satisfactory to the Probate Court, and have mailed a notice to known creditors, so that any party with a potential claim may file with the court. Note that you are not necessarily required to send creditors certified copies of a death certificate unless it is expressly requested by the creditor. Also, note that in the probate process you are never allowed to send notices directly to known creditors. The probate code requires mailed notices be performed by a duly authorized 3rd party representative, such as your attorney.

- Arrangements for all final debts of the estate that are legally required by statute must be made. Note that the legal requirement does not necessarily mean *all* claims that were made must be paid. It is not your obligation to make sure that everyone proves up their claims. If a creditor's claim is not proven to the court's standard, no payment should be made. Your fiduciary obligation is to the estate, not the creditors of the estate.

Once you have performed your statutory minimum requirements, my advice is to stop there. There are lots of books that provide advice which, in my opinion, does more harm than good. Why give away the estate's assets unnecessarily? Why pay claims that are not proven to the court's standards? Why do more than the absolute minimum required by law?

When you act in the capacity of a personal representative or trustee of an estate, you will have some exposure to personal liability. If you commit acts of fraud or gross negligence, you may be held responsible. Even if you do your level best to be scrupulously honest, there is still no guarantee that someone won't sue you. In today's litigious environment, someone who feels that they didn't get a fair shake could very easily hire an attorney and go after you personally. If you didn't start out by hiring a good attorney, guess what? Now you're really going to need one.

If you have taken the advice offered in this book to heart, and have employed the services of a licensed fiduciary, that person will likely be able to work with creditors and claimants to negotiate reduced payments from the estate. Licensed fiduciaries work on a strictly business arrangement - it's nothing personal. Indeed, I deal with estates all the time that are asset rich but cash poor. If you're in that position, you (or your representative) truly have an obligation to try and negotiate a reduction of all estate debts. If you can avoid putting yourself in legal jeopardy or avoid having to make moral judgments about which debts may be valid and which may not, that would be your best course of action.

To wrap up the estate, you'll need to ask your attorney to file a petition with the court for final distribution. If you have accurately done all of the steps noted above, and your attorney agrees that your paperwork is in order, the court will likely approve your petition. At that point, your next step will be to get the transfer documents needed to distribute proceeds to the approved heirs and beneficiaries of the estate. Once that step is complete, and the final fiduciary tax return should be prepared and filed with the IRS. Once that final fiduciary return is accepted as complete, you're done!

THINGS THAT MAY FALL THROUGH THE CRACKS

As long as you have diligently complied with the above steps to the best of your ability, you generally need not concern yourself that some things may have fallen through the cracks. Suppose a creditor comes forward to make a claim six months after the case was opened, even if the claim is valid, do you have an obligation to the estate to refuse the claim? Yes. If the creditor was given proper notice and they missed the deadline, it's not your problem; it's theirs.

In my experience, small things do get overlooked in probate cases all the time. Sometimes previously unknown assets are discovered after the probate case was closed. Sometimes a mistake is found in the accounting. If you are unable to sell an asset because of the way title is held, for example, you may need to go back to the Probate Court and provide evidence that a mistake was made. Such things usually get picked up when people try to liquidate an asset, only to discover that they can't because title is still held in the name of a deceased person. Even if the mistake is discovered 20 years later, a new filing to reopen an old probate case may still be required.

I have also seen people try to avoid probate entirely by pretending that they don't need to bother. A parent may die leaving very few assets, and the child or children beneficiaries decide not to file a probate. Guess what? When they decide it's time to sell the old house which is still in the name of the deceased parent, they discover they can't get title insurance, a very common requirement for buyers of real property. Probate Courts usually don't look kindly on people in such cases.

Ignorance of the law will not provide a legitimate excuse for ignoring the law. Indeed, I have seen many probate estates opened for people who died decades earlier. Without a doubt, in cases big or small where things slipped between the cracks, it is always essential to consult directly with a qualified attorney.

CHAPTER SUMMARY:

- If you have assembled a good team around you, i.e., an attorney, a licensed fiduciary, a CPA, a bookkeeper, a private investigator and real estate professional (realtor and/or appraiser), those professionals will advise you when it's time to wrap up a probate matter.
- Don't be concerned if something unexpected falls through the cracks.
- If it's absolutely necessary, your attorney can always re-open a probate case if such a move is warranted.

Special Needs Trusts

Every family faces unique challenges and hardships. Life is complex and unpredictable, people are fallible and vulnerable, and inevitably some people are better than others at managing their own affairs. Elderly parents often recognize that one or more of their adult children will need help after they're gone, and they want some way to address the problem. It turns out that for parents in this situation there is only one solution: It's called a Special Needs Trust, and it is usually established for the benefit of a single beneficiary, often someone with a problem: Alcoholism, drug addiction, gambling addiction, spending addiction, poor impulse control or any manner of self-destructive behavior.

I first learned about the creation of a Special Needs Trust when I agreed to serve as the successor trustee to my mother's trust when she felt she could no longer competently manage her affairs. Five years before my mother died, she wisely had her attorney prepare an Amendment and Restatement of Trust to address her concern for one of my siblings who suffer from addiction. A Trust Amendment is a legal document that changes specific provisions of a Revocable Living Trust but leaves all the other provisions unchanged, while an Amendment and Restatement of Trust completely replaces and supersedes all the provisions of the original Revocable Living Trust.

When my mother resigned as the settlor trustee and I became her successor trustee, her Amendment and Restatement of Trust had several paragraphs outlining numerous requirements concerning my brother's ability to access assets left to him in our mother's will and her trust:

- My brother's share of beneficial interest in the trust was to be managed by me; my name was used as the person who would manage his inheritance.
- The language in the restated trust concerning how and when my brother would be able to qualify to manage his own inheritance was very detailed. There were descriptive narratives concerning sobriety that created benchmarks for my brother to achieve before he would be allowed to take title to and manage any incremental percentage interests in his inheritance.

Yet, nowhere in the paragraphs of our mother's Amendment and Restatement of Trust were the words "Special Needs Trust" used. I had no idea that a special needs trust was being created in the language used in her new trust amendment and restatement, and I had no idea she had created a legal Special Needs Trust until after she died. When the trust attorney I was working with after my mother's death explained to me that the conditions set forth in our mother's restatement of trust made me the trustee for my brother, I felt like Bill Murray in the movie, Ground Hog Day. After caring for my mother's affairs for five years I looked forward to no longer having that burden, but alas, I was simply changing parties. My tenure as a trustee was not ending as I had expected it would. In fact, it wasn't ending at all. I was shocked to discover that I had literally been made to be my brother's keeper.

I admit to feeling depressed at the idea that I was faced with applying to the Internal Revenue Service for another tax identification number for my brother's trust that was automatically created when my mother died. I was indeed faced with the prospect of having to file annual fiduciary tax returns on behalf of my brother. My brother was caught as flat-footed as me when I made it known to him that he had no powers to access his inheritance. He was not happy, I was not happy, but there was no other possible course of action.

Since the day when I discovered that I had been "sentenced" to become my brother's trustee, I have been exposed to, and even been a party to the creation of Special Needs Trusts in the services I provide as a consultant to trustees in matters of trust litigation in Probate Court and elder financial abuse cases in civil court. It turns out to be a very good idea.

WHY CAREGIVERS ARE OFTEN SUBSTANCE ABUSERS

I work closely with a law firm that specializes in prosecuting elder financial abuse cases. My role in elder financial abuse cases is always related to matters involving real property owned by the trust because that is my area of expertise, although I am not an attorney. Attorneys are rarely experts in real property. They may know the law, but not the practices. Therefore, my knowledge of real property, management of real property and being an Officer of the Court, because I serve as a Court Appointed Receiver in matters of litigation, can be very helpful in the discovery of information needed to prosecute wrongdoers.

My experience in elder financial abuse cases is there is often a family member with substance abuse problems, or gambling addiction, or both. The typical scenario is the addicted family member stays close to an elderly person near the end of their life to "care" for them. This arrangement evolves because the family members who do not suffer from addiction usually have their own families, and busy lives prevent them from spending a lot of time with parents or loved ones who require help or assistance at the end of their lives.

When you have an addict 'helping' an elderly person with diminished capacity, or no capacity, the opportunity to take advantage is simply too easy, and the addict will often run amuck with the opportunity to steal property, money, even obtain Power of Attorney to 'help' their parent or loved one. Addicts are crafty. They manipulate to feed their addiction and they usually lack good judgment or scruples.

The addict is often allowed full access to the elderly parent's finances for years before it is discovered by other family members who are horrified to find that their parents have been financially abused. The result is that siblings' rightful inheritances are decimated. Correcting this abuse in law is easier today thanks to strengthening Federal Standards for Elder Abuse. If you find yourself discovering that your sibling who doesn't have a job and took care of mom has been stealing money, selling property and keeping the proceeds, you are able to seek remedies and equitable justice if you retain competent legal counsel to help you.

ELDER FINANCIAL ABUSE & SPECIAL NEEDS TRUSTS
How is elder financial abuse and Special Needs Trusts related? Often the person who commits elder financial abuse requires their own protection, especially if they have or will inherit from a trust or the probate estate. Attorneys can create Special Needs Trusts to save these people, the impaired beneficiaries, from themselves. However, be aware they cannot be over the age of 65; in such cases, there are other kinds of Trusts that an attorney can set up.

This is how it will typically happen:

- Let's assume you consult with an attorney who agrees your sibling or family member committed elder financial abuse, so you filed an action and settled the litigation against the wrongdoer.

- The wrongdoer will probably be required to make restitution at some level as a condition of the settlement with the beneficiaries of the estate. If, after that restitution, the wrongdoer will still inherit, they are not likely to be competent in managing their finances, especially if they refuse to seek treatment.

Even if wrongdoers who commit elder financial abuse do seek treatment and get sober, recidivism in addiction is very high, and chances are the addict will lapse from sobriety at some time.

Addiction is a disease, so I strongly believe that humane settlements in law for cases of elder financial abuse should include subsequent protections for the wrongdoer who suffers from addiction. Creation of a Special Needs Trust or other mechanisms is an excellent vehicle to accomplish guidelines that will preserve and protect the assets of the addicted or those who lack sufficient capacity in other areas to properly care for themselves. And, a special needs trust is not as draconian or as expensive as having the person conserved in the court system.

Creation of Special Needs Trusts is not common because they apply to specific situations, and they usually require long-term commitments on the part of those who will administer the Trust. If the trust beneficiary has decades of life expectancy, this will be a very substantial commitment in and of itself. In my own case, if I had known what my mother was signing me up for, I probably would have declined. No, I would not have willingly chosen to (literally) be my brother's keeper. My mother knew I was dependable, honest and responsible, so she appointed me. I am not, however, convinced that springing it on someone is the best way to persuade someone to take on the job.

OPTION B: HIRE A LICENSED FIDUCIARY

If you recognize the need to create such a trust, the question you must ask yourself is:

- Do I have a trusted relative who is young enough and has the tenacity to care for your family member for the long-haul?

If the answer is no, the best option is to hire an experienced and knowledgeable licensed professional fiduciary. A licensed professional fiduciary has special skills to administer long-term special needs trusts. They will save you from the burden to care for others you do not have time, or interest, in taking on. Why do that? Because making provisions to protect the abuser from squandering their own resources is always the right thing to do.

The definition of a fiduciary is a person who holds a legal or ethical relationship of trust with one or more other parties. Fiduciaries exist, and their services are employed throughout the United States, Canada, England and Australia. Here in the U.S., some states require fiduciaries to complete minimum course requirements, sit for and pass a licensing exam to receive their fiduciary license. Fiduciaries in California, where I live and work, must hold a professional fiduciary license that is administered by the Professional Fiduciaries Bureau Department of Consumer Affairs.

Typically, a fiduciary in the context we are talking about in this book manages or takes care of money or other assets for another person. Or, they may act in guardianship capacity for other persons who lack capacity to properly care for themselves. In a fiduciary relationship, one person, in a position of vulnerability, endows confidence, good faith, reliance, and trust in another whose justifiable aid, advice, and, or, protection is sought. When such a relation is formed, good conscience requires the fiduciary to act always for the sole benefit and interest of the one who trusts.

Fiduciaries may act as court-appointed trustees, conservators, probate administrators to administer probate estates, and special needs trustees for persons who require periodic oversight in their daily lives. Fiduciaries also perform services for attorneys in litigation, such as agreeing to be court appointed as Substitution Trustee in trust estates where there is conflict, and a neutral party is needed to administer the trust.

Private parties can also hire fiduciaries to assist with administering probate and trust estates. As a Probate Executor or Successor Trustee, you have the right to hire qualified professionals to administer an estate. This option of hiring a licensed fiduciary to assist you or your loved one who is charged with administering a probate or a trust estate is one the "best trick" advice items I will give to you in this book. Hiring a licensed fiduciary to help you administer a trust or probate estate is just like hiring other professionals, and they can help make quicker work of administering and eventually distributing, estate assets to rightful heirs and beneficiaries. If nothing else, fiduciaries have lots of good contacts to help you get through almost any situation. Indeed, licensed fiduciaries often turn to people like me to help in special situations. I am often hired to perform real property management, construction consulting, land use consulting, and to list and sell real property assets.

HOW DO FIDUCIARIES GET PAID?

In the situations where fiduciaries act as special trustees for special needs trust, and as court-appointed conservators, they may be paid a percentage value based upon the value of the trust - say an annual fee equal and fraction percent of the gross value of the trust assets, similar to a commission. More frequently, fiduciaries I work with all over California bill hourly for their services. Billing rates tend to range between $125 - $175 per hour, which is a lot less than attorney rates, but not inexpensive. However, keep in mind; as you get better at doing something you get paid less for doing it.

What does that mean? When you first learn to do something, it takes time to perform that task. As you repeatedly perform that same task, it will take less time. When you bill by the hour, working more efficiently and faster results in less income per task. I point this out so that you won't focus as much on the hourly rate but instead to look at the entire value proposition a professional brings to the table. The limiting condition of remuneration for you acting as a probate executor or trustee is you will never receive approval from the court, or beneficiaries to be paid what the job is worth, so you are well served to employ others who can do it faster and more efficiently than you can. This is an absolute truth.

How do you select and engage a licensed fiduciary? Much the same as hiring an attorney, contractor, or real estate broker; you interview them, obtain references, check online reviews, and then negotiate the services you are seeking and price for services to be rendered.

FIDUCIARIES IN LITIGATION
In matters of conflict with estates, including matters of litigation, fiduciaries will often hire their own legal counsel to advise and protect themselves. An example of this would be when a good trust attorney is seeking to remove a bad trustee. The trustee might be incompetent in performing their duties, or perhaps perpetrated undue influence upon an elderly or others without capacity, that attorney will file with the court to seek a Substitute Trustee. Courts will be more amenable to granting such a petition if the attorney offers to employ a licensed fiduciary, especially one the court is familiar with and known to be competent. The court will issue an order removing the "bad" trustee and appointing the licensed fiduciary as the substitute trustee. Assuming the litigants are not getting along, the fiduciary will condition their acceptance of taking on the role of substitute trustee or substitute probate

administrator in matters of probate, upon having their own legal counsel representation. In those situations, you will be paying the fiduciary their hourly rates as well as their attorney's hourly rate. As we all know, litigation is very expensive, but sometimes it is the necessary choice to make when wrongdoers have taken advantage.

WHEN FIDUCIARIES BECOME ABUSERS

If you are in the position of an executor or trustee where a family member or loved one lacks capacity at a level where they are unable to care for themselves, the often-employed solution is to seek the appointment of a guardian. That process of guardianship appointment is known as conservatorship; the two terms are often used interchangeably. Conservatorship is a legal concept in the United States. A guardian or a protector is appointed by a judge to manage the financial affairs, health care decisions, and/or daily life activities of another due to physical or mental limitations, lack of capacity, age-related health issues such as dementia or Alzheimer disease.

Unfortunately, those who are trained to protect and act in trust sometimes are bad actors themselves, and they can easily steal and take advantage because their court appointments give them unfettered access to assets, management of assets, and care for the vulnerable. It happens more often in matters involving court-appointed conservatorship because conservatorships are often long-term appointments. Trust and probate estates are short-term, even though they often will last 12-18 months or more, it's a series of tasks that end with a distribution of assets and filing a final tax return for the estate. Conservatorships often last a lifetime.

If you are in a position where you may be considering the option of seeking a conservatorship for a family member or loved one whom you are unable to properly care for, please consider reading Dr. Sam Sugar's book entitled, *Guardianships and the Elderly, The Perfect Crime.* Dr. Sugar is the founder of Americans Against Abusive Probate Guardianship. His book outlines how our courts' antiquated system of guardianship is fraught with opportunities for guardians (professional fiduciaries) to mismanage money, over medicate, commit investment fraud, asset theft and fraudulent real estate liquidations to name just a few areas of often reported abuse. The problem is, once you send your loved one down the road of conservatorship, they are lost to the court system, and it is not adequately protecting the vulnerable. Conservatorship can be an extremely useful tool, and there is nothing inherently wrong with the concept, but you do need to be aware of the potential for abuse and to, therefore, be vigilant at all times.

CHAPTER SUMMARY:

- Special Needs Trusts are not common, but they do serve a useful purpose.
- If you are in the position of having to administer a trust which will take care of one or more individuals with very specific and special needs, you should consider hiring a licensed and professional fiduciary, especially if the job would create a time or emotional burden on you.

ACKNOWLEDGMENTS

I became exposed to administering trust and probate estates from being the sibling who was required to administer my parents' separate estates. It was a horrible, confusing task – both times. My father's estate was handled through probate, and my mother's estate was settled through a Trust. After going through my second estate administration, I knew there had to be an easier way to approach this messy, complex, and time-consuming business of settling the life affairs of others. My estate attorney would give me advice; then my CPA would give me what seemed like conflicting advice, then my siblings gave me their nickel's worth of advice and their respective demands while I was left to work out the execution of the disparate interests by myself. I truly wish I had someone like me today, who knows how to execute the steps to settling an estate in a reasonable amount of time to help me back then.

As I reflect to late 1983, my first job in real estate with Ned Eichler, son to one of the San Francisco Bay Area's largest regional developers, Joe Eichler of Eichler Homes, to this day in 2018 I see that I owe acknowledgment to many people who helped me arrive at where I am today. Ned Eichler taught me the commercial correspondent lending business and how to properly evaluate income property, first by focusing on everything but the property: Ned wanted to know what the surrounding properties were, e.g., retail, multi-family, office, their uses, their physical condition, proximity to amenities supporting the subject property, public transportation lines, etc., the last thing Ned wanted to hear about was the actual property I was sent to inspect. Ned was a developer and business leader whom I had as a lecturer in a real estate development course I took at the Business School while I was an undergraduate at U.C. Berkeley. Ned taught that real estate development course to us by telling us actual stories of how he and his family used worked through the conflicting conditions of institutional lenders to keep their home development projects on schedule and keep the loan funds flowing to build and sell homes in multi-phased development projects. Someday in my emeritus future, I hope to be able to impart what I have learned in over three decades of land development to young people too.

To Harvey Solveson the first person who trusted me with my first legal conversion of a warehouse in Oakland into Live Work for artists, your faith allowed me to develop into seasoned developer capable of re-purposing functionally obsolete properties. I served on the City of Oakland's Citizen Committee for Live Work Zoning and Building Code Guidelines with an architect by the name of Tom Dolan. Tom taught me how to use zoning and building codes to develop reasonable standards for converting functionally obsolete buildings into highly useful housing and work studios for visual and musical artists.

I learned land use and land development from Dave Young, a Seattle area developer who allowed me to entitle land, design the project improvements of streets, sidewalks and curbs with civil engineers and build over 100 homes for him in Bend, Oregon, making me into a seasoned land developer and general contractor. My mentor in San Francisco, commercial real estate broker Robert "Bob" Tuller whose infectious energy and countless connections taught me the net leased single tenant sales business selling credit tenant properties all over the United States which later led me into the "build-to-suit" warehouse business for companies like GE Appliance, Big O Tires, and CVS. Tuller and his core group of brokers at BT Commercial Net Leased Sales Group in San Francisco worked as a team for over 40 years of success by doing the same things that worked, over and over, they inspired me to simply follow good examples of work ethic.

My property management experience is owed to several people. Danny Benvenuti, my former partner in residential and warehouse developments, gave me the opportunity to manage a large portfolio of industrial properties for his real estate development business. Those seven years serving as his Executive Vice President gave me a solid foundation to later serve as a property manager over large portfolios in litigation and to develop expertise in best practices. Ben McGrew, 2018 Institute of Real Estate Management (IREM) President, taught me the business of working as a court-appointed Receiver. Since 2009 I worked with Stephen Donell, CPM, CCIM, and "uber receiver" with over 700 cases of receiverships to his credit on many complex receivership cases where we have protected and preserved income property assets involved in litigation.

Andy Fetyko and Chris Zubiate, operators of licensed care facilities throughout California, started as tenants of mine in a commercial care home facility that I re-developed after buying it from a lender who had foreclosed upon it. I have worked with these guys for years, and they taught me the world of care homes; I became a California Certified Residential Care Facility for the Elderly (RCFE) Administrator where I learned the ropes of how vulnerable older adults become and how they are preyed upon. It opened my eyes to a world where our elders are dependent upon others as they age. Congress and states have passed strong laws in recent years to protect vulnerable elders, but those strong laws are not yet being defended or prosecuted by most district attorneys and law enforcement at federal and state levels. Hopefully, this trend will soon shift, and we will see resources of attorneys general and law enforcement begin to enforce the good laws passed to protect the vulnerable aged population in our country.

Michael Hackard, a good friend, and trust estate litigator has given me the opportunity to help his clients in matters involving real property in his trust litigation practice. This has allowed me to be exposed to many situations that develop in estates being poorly managed, or where there are wrongdoers that have taken advantage of elderly adults, and often their siblings' inheritance. The consulting work I do for Mike and his firm's attorneys is where I have developed my best ideas to simplify the estate administration process. I cannot thank him enough.

Some of the attorneys I have worked with and clients who have employed me; Matthew Talbot, Esq. of Talbot Law Group, PC in Walnut Creek, CA encouraged me to do this book. Debra Rose, of Rose Fiduciary & Trust, Licensed Professional Fiduciary and partner in many cases I have worked, you have my appreciation and thanks for your encouragement and advisory contributions to my manuscript. To Adrianne Kordelos who hired me to assist her with a trust estate, she has become a good friend and counsel. To Darleah and Dwayne Cox who also hired me and trusted me to serve as a court appointed Receiver in their trust estate matter, my gratitude is deep. My Certified Public Accountant, Dawn Cornelius of Cornelius & Davini, LLP in Sacramento, she is an absolute gem and she has been a generous resource to serve my clients with measured, practical advice.

The good news is that my background allowed me to learn enough to develop this unique niche of administering estates, thanks to all my mentors. Taking these learned skills and creating a book was due to my friend and publishing mentor, J.P. Mark, researcher, and financial consultant, who has assisted me, and other disparate professionals, in writing a book. I never considered myself to be a writer, and trust me, it is not something I would be able to do alone. J.P. worked tirelessly with me on developing the stories and outlines in this book. This book would never have been published without J.P. Mark's sustained effort to keep me on track in developing the book chapters.

I hope this book helps people who have been tasked with administering estates of loved ones, and for professionals who are tasked to administer estates for people they never met in life, to get through the necessary steps to settle an estate correctly, efficiently, and to successfully execute their fiduciary duties. For those of you who are lucky enough to live in California where I hold my real estate and general contractor license, you are always free to contact me for services to assist with your estate administration needs.

Index

Made in the USA
Middletown, DE
23 February 2019